September 15, 2011

D0400942

PENGUIN BOOKS

I Don't Know What I Want, But I Know It's Not This

Julie Jansen has made five career changes within the broadcasting, contingency recruiting, outplacement, and training industries in order to find work that fulfills and satisfies her professional and personal needs. Currently, she offers coaching and consulting to individuals and companies to help them be successful in their work. Jansen has been featured in publications such as the WSJ.com *Career Journal, Fortune, Working Woman, Psychology Today, New York Post,* and *Redbook,* and she writes articles and gives career advice for *Yahoo!HotJobs, JobDig.com, and Cancerandcareers.org.* A frequent speaker for associations, nonprofit groups, and corporations throughout the United States, she lives in Stamford, Connecticut.

For more information, visit the author's Web site at www.juliejansen.net.

I Don't Know What I Want, But I Know It's Not This

*A Step-by-Step Guide
to Finding Gratifying Work*

JULIE JANSEN

PENGUIN BOOKS

PENGUIN BOOKS
Published by the Penguin Group
Penguin Group (USA) Inc., 375 Hudson Street,
New York, New York 10014, U.S.A.
Penguin Group (Canada), 90 Eglinton Avenue East, Suite 700, Toronto,
Ontario, Canada M4P 2Y3 (a division of Pearson Penguin Canada Inc.)
Penguin Books Ltd, 80 Strand, London WC2R 0RL, England
Penguin Ireland, 25 St Stephen's Green, Dublin 2,
Ireland (a division of Penguin Books Ltd)
Penguin Group (Australia), 250 Camberwell Road, Camberwell,
Victoria 3124, Australia (a division of Pearson Australia Group Pty Ltd)
Penguin Books India Pvt Ltd, 11 Community Centre,
Panchsheel Park, New Delhi–110 017, India
Penguin Group (NZ), 67 Apollo Drive, Rosedale, North Shore 0632,
New Zealand (a division of Pearson New Zealand Ltd)
Penguin Books (South Africa) (Pty) Ltd, 24 Sturdee Avenue,
Rosebank, Johannesburg 2196, South Africa

Penguin Books Ltd, Registered Offices:
80 Strand, London WC2R 0RL, England

First published in Penguin Books 2003
This revised and updated edition published 2010

1 3 5 7 9 10 8 6 4 2

LIBRARY OF CONGRESS CATALOGING IN PUBLICATION DATA
Jansen, Julie.
I don't know what I want, but I know it's not this : a step-by-step guide
to finding gratifying work / Julie Jansen.—Rev. and updated ed.
p. cm.
Includes bibliographical references and index.
ISBN 978-0-14-311699-8
1. Career changes. 2. Job satisfaction. 3. Career development. I. Title.
HF5384.J36 2010
650.14—dc22   2009035745

Printed in the United States of America
Set in Garamond 3
Designed by Susan Hood

To my brother Dave. I wish you were here.

Acknowledgments

There are so many people in my life who helped me make this book such a success the first time around. You know who you are, and I thank you from the bottom of my heart. For this revised edition I would like to express my gratitude to:

Denise Marcil, my agent, who has always been passionate about this book.

Stephen Morrison, my wonderful publisher, and Becca Hunt, my very supportive editor at Penguin.

Gary, the love of my life, for everything he brings to me and for his fabulous research skills.

All my readers whose loyalty has given me the opportunity to revise this book.

Contents

Introduction   xi

PART I   WHERE ARE YOU NOW?   1

Chapter 1   Why Do You Want or Need to Change Your Work?   3
Chapter 2   What Is Your Work Situation?   11

PART II   WHERE DO YOU WANT TO BE?   25

Chapter 3   Values, Attitudes, and Change Resilience   27
Chapter 4   Personality Preferences, Interests, and Favorite Skills   43

PART III   HOW DO YOU GET THERE?   61

Chapter 5   Where's the Meaning?   63
Chapter 6   Been There, Done That, but Still Need to Earn   87
Chapter 7   Bruised and Gun-shy   102
Chapter 8   Bored and Plateaued   125
Chapter 9   Yearning to Be on Your Own   144
Chapter 10   One Toe in the Retirement Pool   182
Chapter 11   The Eleven Keys to Success   201
Chapter 12   Job Search—the Nuts and Bolts   229

Afterword   251
Resources   257
Index   277

Introduction

The first edition of *I Don't Know What I Want, But I Know It's Not This* was published in 2003. It is seven years later, and there are still so many people who aren't happy, fulfilled, or even moderately satisfied with their work.

In the last few years we have been inundated with the highest unemployment in decades, the largest stock market plummets we've seen in most of our lifetimes, and the demise of U.S. financial institutions and corporations that have previously withstood world wars and the Great Depression of 1929. These events have created working environments filled with fear and mistrust. While most people working are grateful to have a job as they watch their friends and colleagues lose their jobs, their workloads have magnified and their stress has escalated.

While I was first writing this book and someone would ask me what it was about, I'd explain that it was about how to find satisfying work for the rest of your life. Without exception that person would say either "Boy, I sure could use your book right now!" or "My husband [neighbor/sister/son/cousin] desperately needs your book." Years later that refrain hasn't changed one bit, and the need for finding gratifying work is even greater. In fact, in Salary.com's annual 2008/2009 Employee Satisfaction and Retention Survey, it was found that 65 percent of 7,141 individuals surveyed admitted to passively or actively looking for a new job or thinking about starting a business.

Some distinct changes have occurred in the workplace in the last several years, and among them is an even stronger need to define who you are (and aren't) and to find ways to brand yourself in your work. This means becoming well known for something, whether it is a quality, a skill, or a specialty.

Another significant element of looking for a job, changing careers, and working in general is the necessity to be as resilient, nimble, and flexible as possible in order to meet the continuing extraordinary changes that are occurring in companies and in the workplace.

According to the World Future Society's (www.wfs.org) forecasts for 2009 and beyond, careers and the college majors for preparing them are becoming more specialized. This means that instead of simply majoring in business, students are exploring niche majors such as sustainable business, strategic intelligence, digital forensics, and comic book art.

Another World Future Society forecast that has become true in recent years is that professional knowledge becomes obsolete as quickly as it is acquired. An individual's professional knowledge is becoming outdated at the fastest rate it ever has. This requires a continuous need for instruction, education, and retraining.

Finally, the need to develop a strong Internet presence is a must. This means constantly updating your online profiles on LinkedIn, Plaxo, or any social networking Web site of your choice, writing blogs and commenting on blog entries, tweeting, and reaching out to your online connections regularly.

I am now in my fifth career, as a speaker, consultant, and career coach, which has made me even more intrigued by how and why people choose the work they do. I wrote this book to motivate others—to help them feel confident that being happy with work is a choice you *can* and *should* make. I empathize with those who are not happy or satisfied and have had difficult work experiences.

Why? I have had many myself. I have been fired, my job has been eliminated, I have had nasty bosses (two), and I have been caught in mergers and political battles. I have also worked for companies whose cultures were a bad fit for my needs, and I even had an ex-employer threaten to sue me because I had signed a noncompete clause preventing me from working in the same industry. I have been bored, disinterested, unchallenged, and miserable as well as stimulated, engaged, and fulfilled. What did I learn from all these experiences? I learned that discovering the right work gives you motivation and confidence while you build a strong foundation. This enables you to bounce back and renew or even reinvent yourself when you need to do it. And you will need to do it!

This book will show you how to do all these things as you proceed on your journey to gratifying work.

I Don't Know What I Want, But I Know It's Not This

PART I

Where Are You Now?

CHAPTER 1

Why Do You Want or Need to Change Your Work?

"I'm turning forty this year, and all of a sudden I'm questioning what I'm doing workwise. I've never had these feelings before. It's crazy!" says Kim, senior vice president of human resources at one of the largest banks in the United States.

Maybe you can identify with Kim's comment and her feelings of confusion about work. The workplace of today and what is predicted for the future certainly doesn't resemble the workplace that most people entered ten, fifteen, or thirty years ago. And it never will again. For a variety of reasons it has become increasingly difficult for most of us to feel satisfied with our work situation. Louise Lague, a psychotherapist and author, sums it up well: "Technology has made it possible to work all the time from anywhere. This has made many workplaces hell on earth—they never close! Deadlines are tighter, more is expected, and weekends and evenings are consistently interrupted."

The constant changes taking place in companies, including the temporary nature of jobs that were once relatively permanent, create a stressful work environment in which people find it difficult to feel satisfied, let alone happy. Seemingly endless communication (e-mail, instant messaging, texting, tweeting, voice mail, meetings), multiple projects with multiple deadlines, and extreme pressure to increase profits all contribute to an atmosphere in which many workers feel overwhelmed.

Debbie sold nurse-call systems to hospitals for a giant health-care solutions company. She felt so much stress from nonstop travel and unrealistic sales goals that she finally quit, taking a job that didn't have the same upside potential financially but also wouldn't be nearly as stressful. After giving notice at her former company, she spoke with ten or more individuals at various levels in the corporate hierarchy to say good-bye. She was shocked when every one of them told her that she was lucky to be able to quit, and if they felt they could leave their jobs, they would do so immediately. They made comments such as "It's not what it used to be" and "The company doesn't support us anymore; all they care about is profits."

"Burnout is not caused by too much work," Louise Lague explains, "but by working all day on projects that have no meaning to you personally. It takes much more psychic energy to do something you hate than something you love." When you are working at a job that you dislike, these negative feelings take over all your free time, including weekends. Lague continues, "It's entirely likely that projects that once excited us no longer do. We live and grow and keep learning, and when healthy people stop learning, they get bored and yearn to learn something new. It's a mistake to think that there's something wrong with job dissatisfaction—it's absolutely normal and healthy."

Kim, the human resources executive mentioned earlier, works for a bank that acquired two large companies—the eighth acquisition in three years. The greatest problem posed by these acquisitions is the inability of the organization to successfully merge the disparate corporate cultures. This organizational stumbling block has resulted in higher employee turnover and confusion about shared values and goals. Not only has Kim been affected personally, but as a senior human resources executive she also must deal with the serious repercussions that the mergers have on other employees.

Even though people know intellectually that hard work and loyalty aren't important to most employers the way they once were, it is difficult for most of us to accept it on an emotional level, especially the two older generations: baby boomers and veterans. And the massive layoffs that have taken place over the last several years have further decreased the amount of loyalty employees of any age might once have had. The opportunities for advancement that once existed have decreased significantly as well, causing confusion about what to strive for in one's job. This is especially true for the more seasoned worker who in the past was always motivated by working toward his or her next step up the organizational ladder.

Many people are also feeling the stress brought on by multiple generations working together. There are currently four generations working side by side in the workplace, each with conflicting values, attitudes, and expectations. Typically, veterans (born between 1922 and 1943) see work as an obligation, baby boomers (those born between 1946 and 1964) view work as an adventure, Gen Xers (the generation born after the boomers, between 1965 and 1978) approach work as a difficult challenge or contract, and Millennials (also known as Gen Y, born between 1981 and 1994) look at work as a means to an end or a place to find fulfillment. In their book *Generations at Work,* for example, Ron Zemke, Claire Raines, and Bob Filipczak describe the disconnect between baby boomers and Gen Xers: "Boomers see Xers as alternatively greedy and lazy, suspicious and self-serving, loners and cynics." And "Xers, for their part, see Boomers as obsessive, 'my way or the highway,' a little naïve, a little soft." The negative perceptions that each generation has of the other lead to conflict, frustration, and distrust—not the optimal ingredients for a comfortable work environment. Interestingly, this discord in approaches to work has become a major factor for members of all four generations to want to change careers. Surveys that support this premise have been conducted by Fairleigh Dickinson University, *USA Today,* and JobDig.com.

Many people over the age of forty are feeling increasingly dissatisfied because they are experiencing either subtle or blatant discrimination from their employers. Joanie, at fifty-two, has sold advertising time in television for her entire career. When she was fifty years old, her boss stripped her of her national sales manager title and responsibilities, telling her, "You're fifty now and shouldn't be traveling as much." Many people in their forties and fifties believe that businesses are more interested in the young and technologically savvy worker. In particular, people who were laid off in their late forties and fifties are, in many instances, convinced that their age had a lot to do with the decision. People in this age range believe that companies, especially large corporations, perceive workers older than forty-five as less creative, less flexible, and more expensive than younger employees.

And, indeed, there is ample evidence that older employees are often replaced by young people who are willing to work like crazy. When these younger workers become managers, it can and often does lead to discomfort or outright conflict with older employees who once held these same jobs. The bottom line? Older employees often don't want to stay with companies where they are perceived in a negative light simply because of their age.

—————

Yet another reason employees feel frustrated and dissatisfied is that most corporations, whether large or small, still manage their employees based on the old "bricks-and-mortar" model in which "everyone works in one place." Many companies either can't figure out how to design a new model or are changing very slowly to support different lifestyle needs and create a flexible workforce. People get frustrated with this slow pace and increasingly are going to work for savvy companies who they think meet their employees' needs in this area. Ben, for example, designed audio equipment for a small company, commuting 112 miles every day for three years. Even though he could be very productive working in his home office, his employer didn't believe in telecommuting, thinking that if an employee wasn't in his company office, he wasn't working. Although Ben loved his job, his boss, and the company overall, at forty-seven he wanted to eliminate or at least reduce the stress of a long commute. He found a job with a larger audio company and now works from home. When he gave notice to his employers, in an attempt to keep him they grudgingly agreed to allow Ben to work at home once a week. While it was tempting to stay, Ben knew they never would fully support him, and he accepted the new job. As he anticipated, he feels healthier, and the stress created by driving a long distance to work every day is gone.

In today's work climate more and more individuals are questioning the grueling pace at which they lead their lives. A 2007 survey by human resource consulting firm Mercer showed that American workers get much less vacation than most other countries, ranking 37 out of 49 nations. Despite this, one in three Americans doesn't use all his allotted vacation time, and whatever time he does take off is used in slices, according to consulting firm Hewitt Associates. Verizon surveyed its employees about working while on vacation, and half admitted they either call in to work or check their e-mail while away on vacation. And according to a Families and Work Institute study, 16 percent of those surveyed bring work home more than once a week. What does all this prove?

Psychologically, the concept of introducing balance into one's life seems far-fetched and unrealistic for many workers. Why? The demands of today's workplace are excessive for most people. With technology allowing twenty-four-hour communication, employees feel obligated to work all the time, whether it be on weekends or on vacation. Even more important, many companies that have policies that support balance can give employees a mixed message about whether it is acceptable to leave the office at a reasonable hour or take all the vacation and personal time allotted in the company employee handbook. If senior management and the corporate culture demonstrate that succeeding means working around the clock, then the pressure of fitting in and "doing what it takes to get the job done" can override the desire to lead a balanced life.

In most cases the challenge of creating a more balanced work life does not mean stopping work. Regardless of age, many of us feel that our sense of self is wrapped up in our work, and psychologically it would be difficult to stop working altogether even if we could afford to do so financially. The financial need to work is primary for most people. In *Age Works*, Beverly Goldberg explains that when Social Security legislation was enacted in the mid-1930s, the average life expectancy was a bit less than sixty-two years, with individuals older than sixty-five comprising only 7 percent of the population. By contrast, according to U.S. Census Bureau projections, a substantial increase in the number of people over sixty-five will occur during the 2010 to 2030 period, after the first baby boomers turn sixty-five in 2011. The older population in 2030 is projected to grow to 72 million, representing 20 percent of the total U.S. population.

A multitude of financial implications flow from these statistics. People rely on Social Security, pensions, and personal savings to finance retirement. Many people are not confident, however, that Social Security as we know it today will continue to exist in the future. As for retirement plans, before the recession of 2008, 55 percent of Americans who were employed by companies were not covered by an employer-provided retirement plan. Projections show that corporations are stopping 401(k) matches for those employees who are fortunate to have this benefit, and equity assets in retirement plans continue to drop dramatically.

In addition, baby boomers, who comprise the largest segment of the working population, are notorious for their poor saving habits, and a large percentage have had their 401(k) plans decimated in the recent stock market decline. Because of this, many of us will find ourselves working longer and retiring later than previous generations.

People are also dissatisfied for reasons that don't necessarily have to do with the company they work for or the workplace overall.

Instead, they have found themselves, either gradually or suddenly, feeling discontented or disenchanted with their work. Such feelings have more to do with the individuals themselves than with how they feel about their employer, and they may stem either from inner conflicts or from a longing for something different.

It is no longer true that the majority of people who question whether their values and goals are being met are middle-aged. Although many events that typically occur in midlife—such as the death of a parent or a child leaving for college—may cause us to think more clearly about what is important to us, there is no age limit on searching for happiness and fulfillment in work and life. The recession of 2008 has caused many people in their twenties and thirties to examine what they need and want from work.

Although many employees are unhappy in their work, some of these people probably don't even know *why* they are unhappy, yet they acutely feel the symptoms of their discontent. These feelings can range from being depressed, bored, lethargic, and apathetic to being overwhelmed, stressed, or unchallenged. Those who do understand the reasons for their dissatisfaction are usually stuck; they find it easier to remain in an unhappy work situation than learn how to "unstick" themselves.

Work in the twenty-first century is dramatically different from the way it was in the 1960s, 1970s, 1980s, and early to mid-1990s. Engaging in a single career or lifelong trade is no longer the way we work or will work in the future. The U.S. Department of Labor estimates that the average American will have three to five careers in his or her lifetime and ten to twelve jobs, and will hold each job an average of three and a half years. This means that changing careers is not only acceptable, it is expected. Additionally, according to the Bureau of Labor Statistics, in 2009 more than 7.7 million people held more than one job, an increase of nearly 300,000 from the recession of 2001. The demands of the marketplace as well as our personal lifestyle choices dictate the kind of work we do and the way we structure it. Because of this, the capacity to shift gears more easily where work is concerned has become a critical skill for those intent on achieving a significant measure of life satisfaction. Learning to master this ability and make it your own will alleviate much of the discomfort and pain you may have experienced in the past or are feeling now.

Living is about making choices. Deciding what kind of work will make you happy is a choice—a big one. Today there are so many choices that sometimes it may seem easier to sit still and not make any at all. But you have a clear choice: You can decide either to begin the process of change or continue doing something that isn't making you happy.

This book is about learning how to identify and create work that is right for you. The odds are that once you've read this book and have decided that you are ready and committed to change your work, you will look for a new job or career, and possibly leave the kind of work you've been doing for many years. Whatever you decide to do, there is one important point to bear in mind: Work is not "one size fits all." Your ability to make smart choices about the kind of work you do depends very much on who you are as an individual.

Every person I work with as a career coach feels unhappy or unfulfilled in his or her work or career. These people often tell me that many of their colleagues feel the same way but are resigned to their situation or are not sure how to change it—so they don't. This is frequently the case given the pervasive job insecurity that the recession of 2008 has created. It is not abnormal or wrong to feel dissatisfied with work, but if you are feeling consistently negative about it, it is a mistake *not* to make changes in your work.

Now it's time to move ahead and begin your journey toward a life of satisfying work!

CHAPTER 2

What Is Your Work Situation?

Six work situations represent a specific contemporary work-life challenge that you may be facing right now. Reading about these work situations will enable you to label and isolate the reasons for your desire to change your work and, in doing so, gain a clearer understanding of how to alleviate your dissatisfaction or discontent. While you probably will relate to one of the six work situations more than the others, it is highly likely that you will identify with two or three of them. These situations are as follows:

1. *Where's the Meaning?* These individuals are looking for a new kind of reward and satisfaction. They may be seeking personal fulfillment or be driven by a strong desire to help others in need. Bill, for example, was an engineer for fifteen years but never really enjoyed his work. After being downsized by his company, a telephone equipment reconditioning business, Bill took some time off and did some volunteer work for five different organizations. He currently earns money by working several part-time jobs. His wife volunteers for many of the same organizations, and Bill tells me that they are both happier and having more fun than they ever had when they were earning substantially more money.

2. *Been There, Done That, but Still Need to Earn.* These people have been, and continue to be, successful in their work. They want and probably need to keep earning at the same level, yet they can't conceive of staying in the same job for another ten or twenty years. Many of these individuals won't be able to change careers immediately, but with planning they can do so eventually. A prime example is Melinda, who has worked as a computer systems programmer for most of her career. She stayed where she was for a while because she was making good money and because financial responsibilities precluded her from changing. When her children were older, she began to work as a personal fitness trainer at night and on weekends. Once Melinda's life situation changed (her children grew up, and she divorced her husband), she was able to launch full-time into her personal training business with established clients. Today she is making very close to the same amount of money doing something she enjoys.

3. *Bruised and Gun-shy.* These individuals are victims of the changing workplace. Having been laid off or discriminated against, they are hesitant to either join the corporate world again or take any kind of career risk, and yet they do need to continue working. Juan, after being laid off, had a quadruple bypass during the transition period and decided to become what he calls a "job stress coach." Ambivalent about reentering the corporate world, he now has his own practice helping others deal with the stress of working. In 2008 and 2009 enormous numbers of people were laid off from their jobs, and most of them remained unemployed months later. Those people who haven't lost their jobs are constantly looking over their shoulders, wondering if they will be a job loss casualty soon.

4. *Bored and Plateaued.* Many people have worked hard for many years and are simply ready to make a change because they are bored and are looking for new challenges. Deborah, at forty, had spent her entire career in consumer-products marketing. A vice president at an elite marketing firm, she admitted that she was "bored to tears." She remembered the early years of her career as being exciting and fun. For at least four years, however, she had felt stagnant, and finally she became so miserable that she decided to actively seek a new direction.

5. *Yearning to Be on Your Own.* These people dream of being on their own or starting a company. According to Helen Harkness, author of *Don't Stop the Career Clock*, in the early nineteenth century, 80 percent of Americans were self-employed. By 1970 this number had fallen to 9 percent. But today self-employment is growing at a furious pace: In 2000 there were 12 million small businesses. According to SBA.gov, in 2007 small firms represented 99.7 percent of all employer firms, totaling 27.2 million small businesses. Another type of self-employment is the "contingency workforce"—people who work temporarily on specific projects for many different companies; these comprised 13.8 percent of the workforce in the United States in 2009. These workers don't have many of the responsibilities that a business owner has, yet they possess the flexibility that people experience in their own businesses. Some contingency workers receive benefits, and some don't. With the increased stress of working for a company, more and more people are realizing that working on their own can satisfy their specific needs. After spending thirty successful years in teaching, sales, and human resources, Blanche started her own consulting firm several years ago. She says, "I always knew I wanted my own business and to have my stamp on something." She is having a lot of fun and has hit every goal she set for herself and her business.

6. *One Toe in the Retirement Pool.* These people are often baby boomers who want to semiretire or retire from their current work. What to do in the years ahead is a question that many boomers are asking themselves: Do they change careers completely, volunteer, scale down the time they are working in their current job, or just retire completely? Di retired when she was fifty-eight from a long career in sales because her exhausting travel schedule was

seriously affecting her health. During the first few years of her retirement she took yoga classes, read books, and learned how to paint in oils. Recently she has started doing some training seminars for a previous employer, and she is enjoying the combination of retirement and part-time work.

Take a few moments and look at the descriptions of the six situations. The following list of questions and statements will help you identify your primary work situation, as well as the others that you fit within, and will provide you with additional clarity about why you associate with a specific circumstance. Taking this assessment may confirm what you already suspect about your reasons for being discontented with your work and allow you to gain further insights.

What Is Your Work Situation?

Read each statement carefully and answer yes or no as quickly and as easily as you can. The statements are grouped by work situation, and while you may think you fit into only one or two categories, you should answer all the statements to get a complete picture of your own circumstance.

WHERE'S THE MEANING?

1. In the last year or so, you have asked yourself, "Why am I doing the work I'm doing?" or "What is the point of the work I do?"

Yes   No

2. I'm not exactly sure what doing meaningful work means to me, but I'd be interested in finding out.

Yes   No

3. It is important that I directly touch or make a contribution to others as often as possible in my work.

Yes   No

4. I am feeling more and more that there is no reward or challenge for doing the work that I do.

Yes   *No*

5. I fantasize about "throwing in the towel" and going to work for a nonprofit organization or a specific cause.

Yes   *No*

6. There are several charities or special causes that I am very interested in learning more about and perhaps getting involved in, even simply as a volunteer.

Yes   *No*

7. My family and friends don't believe that I am making a difference in the world with my work.

Yes   *No*

8. I've experienced a traumatic or sad event in the recent past that has caused me to think about what is really important to me as a person in both my work and life.

Yes   *No*

9. I have an interest or hobby that I am passionate about and that I wish I could become more deeply involved with.

Yes   *No*

10. At one time it was important for me to meet my financial and achievement goals in my work, but this doesn't seem to matter to me anymore.

Yes   *No*

BEEN THERE, DONE THAT, BUT STILL NEED TO EARN

1. My work is no longer providing me with opportunities to do what matters to me, yet I'm used to my income.

Yes   *No*

2. I feel as if I have achieved a lot in my current career and would love to try a different kind of work but am afraid that then I wouldn't earn what I do now.

Yes   No

3. Earning the same amount of money or more is important to me so that I can take care of my family, but I am a little bored.

Yes   No

4. I really enjoy my work but feel as though I've had every possible experience in my career. Despite this, I honestly can't see changing careers because it would probably mean earning less money.

Yes   No

5. I have a lot of financial responsibilities that cause me to feel insecure about changing careers and earning less money.

Yes   No

6. While money is a big reason that I am afraid to change my work, if I think about it, I can find a realistic way to reduce or even eliminate my expenses in the next year or two.

Yes   No

7. I admit that I've been rather bored and unchallenged in my job lately, but I'm hard-pressed to think of anything else I could do and earn the same paycheck.

Yes   No

BRUISED AND GUN-SHY

1. I had a tough job experience that caused me to lose my job and derail my career for a period of time, and I find it difficult to describe my experience or even think about it without feeling anger or other negative emotions.

Yes   No

2. I don't feel optimistic about the future of my career, in part because of my past negative work experiences.

Yes *No*

3. I have been fired at least once. I still feel a little bitter about my experience, and although I'm not thrilled with my work situation, I don't think about making a change for fear it could happen again.

Yes *No*

4. I am unemployed and can't seem to find the energy to focus on finding work that I enjoy, let alone a job of any kind.

Yes *No*

5. I don't trust the corporate world anymore. When I started working, company loyalty was important. Joining a company meant you stayed there forever.

Yes *No*

6. I've experienced some hard knocks in my career. I've been laid off, gotten caught in company politics, been discriminated against, and in one instance my company was sold. How much more do I have to take?

Yes *No*

7. It seems that what companies want from their employees keeps changing. I just don't know if I can keep up the pace any longer, but I can't afford to stop working, either.

Yes *No*

8. I've thought about becoming self-employed or changing careers, but I've been so burned that I'm afraid to make any changes.

Yes *No*

BORED AND PLATEAUED

1. I've been working in the same job for more than two years without a change in responsibilities and can perform my tasks effortlessly without stretching myself.

Yes   No

2. I've invested a lot of time and energy in my work and am considered an expert in my field, yet I feel the need to change something about it, however minor that change may be.

Yes   No

3. I am so busy with tasks and projects that I don't have time to "smell the roses."

Yes   No

4. I have been having trouble getting out of bed in the morning, especially during the week, and feel unmotivated when I'm at work.

Yes   No

5. I daydream about quitting my job and doing something entirely different because I don't feel passionate about my work anymore.

Yes   No

6. At work I am experiencing feelings of burnout (anger, frustration, depression, and anxiety).

Yes   No

7. I guess after so many years in my field I should think about doing something different, but what would I do?

Yes   No

8. Although I know that my peers respect me, I'm starting to wonder if people think I still have passion for my job. In fact, I have been wondering that myself.

Yes   No

9. I moved from another firm in my industry a few years ago in hopes that I would feel reinvigorated. I am starting to feel the way I did before I changed jobs—stale and unstimulated.

Yes   *No*

10. I've just begun to notice that I am not being included in important meetings regarding policy or strategy as often as I used to be. I feel as though I'm not contributing anything new, either.

Yes   *No*

11. Meetings, employees, and clients are all starting to look the same. This feeling scares me, but I'm not sure what to do about it.

Yes   *No*

YEARNING TO BE ON YOUR OWN

1. I no longer feel fulfilled working for someone else and don't think another job will give me what I'm missing now.

Yes   *No*

2. I am increasingly dissatisfied with the way the company I work for is run, and I'm convinced that I can do things differently and better.

Yes   *No*

3. I grew up in an entrepreneurial family or am close to someone who is an entrepreneur. I appreciate the advantages of having my own business more than I fear the disadvantages.

Yes   *No*

4. I'm so envious of people in their own businesses. I know it's not easy, but the thought of being my own boss is so appealing.

Yes   *No*

5. I've always dreamed of being in my own little business. I know there are plenty of resources out there for entrepreneurs, but I am not sure where or how to begin.

Yes   No

6. I know that being on my own doesn't have to mean starting a company. I would like to learn more about my options for self-employment because it is very attractive to me.

Yes   No

7. I know I want to go into business for myself someday but have never been a good salesperson. I'm afraid that not being comfortable with selling will cause me to fail.

Yes   No

8. I have thought a lot about the kind of work I'd like to do next, and I'm convinced that being an entrepreneur is my next move.

Yes   No

9. The idea of being an independent contractor is incredibly appealing.

Yes   No

10. I'm very independent and have always had trouble with politics and working on teams. I am beginning to think that some form of being on my own makes sense for me.

Yes   No

ONE TOE IN THE RETIREMENT POOL

1. The truth is that I really would like to stop working right now. It just seems unrealistic to do so financially.

Yes   No

2. I never want to stop working completely, but I would like to slow my pace down a bit and do something different and less demanding.

Yes   *No*

3. I've been obsessing more and more about not working and spending more time with my family and with my hobbies and interests.

Yes   *No*

4. I'm stressed out from the demands of working and my health isn't what it should be. I'm seriously thinking about retirement.

Yes   *No*

5. I'm worn out from working. I've thought about my alternatives, and partial retirement seems like the best one for me as long as I can work part-time.

Yes   *No*

6. I've worked for a long time and would welcome ideas about structuring the next phase of my life.

Yes   *No*

SCORE KEY

Place a check below next to the categories in which you answered yes to four or more of the statements. Those are the work situations that describe how you feel about work right now.

- ☐ Where's the Meaning?
- ☐ Been There, Done That, but Still Need to Earn
- ☐ Bruised and Gun-shy
- ☐ Bored and Plateaued
- ☐ Yearning to Be on Your Own
- ☐ One Toe in the Retirement Pool

Now it's time to move forward and learn more about yourself and your preferences, needs, and desires—for your work and for your life. Once you have completed the self-assessments in chapters 3 and 4, you may choose to move through this book either sequentially or in a zigzag fashion. Each work situation is discussed in its own chapter with case studies of people who fall into the particular situation.

You will learn a three-step process for leaving your current work situation behind and moving toward something new or different, or merely changing aspects of your work to create what is missing.

Step 1: Complete the Self-Assessments Specific to Your Work Situation

The first logical step to putting a plan together for your career is to learn and understand what your unique values, interests, personality preferences, attitudes, and favorite skills are. By using this information about yourself as a foundation, you'll be better able to focus your job search or career direction. Each of the six work situations requires additional assessments specific to your circumstance and the direction you'd like your career to take.

Step 2: Explore Roadblocks and Opportunities

Many obstacles and barriers may be preventing you from pursuing a different kind of occupation or changing the way you work—for example, age, money, time, education, and a lack of experience. On the positive side, the opportunities are limitless. In this step you will learn how to get around roadblocks and exploit your opportunities.

Step 3: Create an Action Plan

An action plan requires quite a bit of thought and preparation. While creating your plan requires a lot of time and energy, the action plan is an extremely valuable tool to use for mapping out a new career or revamping your career goals.

—————

Although the journey that this book will take you on is not easy, it should be fascinating and eminently worthwhile. Ultimately, it will bring you to your desired destination: satisfying and fulfilling work for as long as you'd like to do it.

PART II

Where Do You Want to Be?

CHAPTER 3

Values, Attitudes, and Change Resilience

Whether you merely want to tweak your work situation or change it dramatically, it is essential that you get to know the one person who will be indispensable to your quest for work that fits: *you*. Understanding who you are—your values, attitudes, preferences, and personality traits—is the key to discovering the kind of work that will bring you personal fulfillment. Here is a simple analogy: If you invite friends over for a home-cooked dinner, you need to know exactly what ingredients to use in preparing the meal. When you throw in just any old ingredients, your guests will leave hungry and disappointed because the food you cooked tasted awful. Your values, personality traits, attitudes, and abilities are like the ingredients of a recipe. Without knowing what they are, you will find it difficult to use these ingredients to help you create nourishing work.

A common mistake that many people make after deciding they are unhappy in their work is to jump immediately into updating their résumé and answering help-wanted ads on the Internet or in the newspaper and to completely overlook the first and very necessary step: self-assessment. According to psychologist Suzanne Roff, director of Compass Point Consulting, LLC, a firm that specializes in career and organizational assessments, "With so many people dissatisfied with the work they do, it's more important than ever to think about job fit. Career assessments help begin an exploration process. There is no one direction for an individual, but some directions are just more viable than others. It often takes gathering more information and getting some help to make an advantageous change."

Bottom line? Don't skip this chapter or chapter 4! Read them, complete the assessments, and refer back to them as you read the rest of the book. In addition to helping you create your ideal work situation, the self-assessment process can help you uncover a whole new repertoire of words, phrases, and concepts that will add a rich new dimension to your résumé and job interviews. Not only will this make you feel more confident and prepared, but it will also have a positive effect on the people who meet you.

Assessment: What It Is and How It Is Used

"Assessment" is a generic term used to describe the various tests, questionnaires, quizzes, surveys, inventories, and checklists used by career counselors, job search consultants, outplacement specialists, coaches, and other career management professionals to assist their clients. Using self-assessments will allow you to collect and evaluate your own preferences, experiences, values, needs, skills, and other personal traits. It is a foundation to help you identify or create the most suitable possible work opportunities for yourself. In other words, self-assessments help you find work that fits. Just imagine how productive the world would be if everyone who works found work that truly suited them.

The assessments in this chapter fall into three categories:

- Values
- Attitudes
- Change Resilience

Some people are fearful or intimidated by the assessment process because of what they may learn about themselves. Let's be perfectly clear: The assessments in this book are not psychological or clinical tests. In no way can a conclusion about your sanity or any personality dysfunction be ascertained from your answers. Self-assessments simply reaffirm what you already know about yourself—whether consciously or not—and provide you with a framework within which to pursue your quest for more satisfying work.

Joan has worked for several years in the search business for an agency recruiting and placing marketing professionals, and has been very happy in her work. Before this she worked as a senior administrative support professional. She truly believes that if she hadn't taken several self-assessment tests after being laid off from her last administrative position, she wouldn't be working in recruiting today. By completing the self-assessment process she was able to decide on a different direction for herself, one that she would never have considered otherwise. "Each person has a distinct personality and specific abilities which need to be guided toward possible career paths that are suitable for that person. When someone's decisions are based on these assessments, there will be a higher degree of success in a particular occupation; therefore, the result is greater fulfillment and happiness because the person is doing what he or she was meant to do in life. I'm living proof of this!" Joan says.

Let's begin your self-assessment process.

Values

A value is defined as a principle, standard, or quality considered inherently worthwhile or desirable. Individuals, groups, and whole societies hold values. Values are what motivate and fulfill you. They imbue your work and your life with meaning. Values can be either personal and non-work-related or completely work-related. In most cases, however, the values that are important to you will inform both your work life and your personal life. In essence, a value is what is important to you. While career psychologists have identified well over one hundred possible values, the list you are about to read contains forty values.

In this assessment you will first identify all the values that are important to you. You will then narrow down the list to your ten most important values. Last, you'll identify which of your top ten values are satisfied in your current work situation. This process will help you understand what is missing now so that you can be clear about what you're not willing to be without in the new work you choose.

Read the following list and place a check mark in the box to the left of each value that is important to you. Check as many as you like. Be careful not to check a value that you think "should" be of importance to you. Check only those you truly live by or are committed to living by in the future. For now, ignore the boxes on the right of each value.

List of Values

- ☐ Achievement/accomplishment: producing results that are significant; completing tasks and projects successfully. ☐
- ☐ Advancement: consistently moving ahead to new and progressive opportunities. ☐
- ☐ Autonomy: ability to choose own projects, set own pace, prepare own schedule, and have own work habits with minimal supervision. ☐
- ☐ Balance: spending equivalent time and effort on tasks, work, and overall life. ☐
- ☐ Belonging to a group: having a sense of being a contributing member of a group. ☐
- ☐ Building something: creating or establishing a thing or idea. ☐
- ☐ Challenge: involvement with stimulating or demanding tasks or projects. ☐
- ☐ Competition: engaging in activities where results are measured frequently and compared with others'. ☐

- ☐ Creativity: making, inventing, or producing innovative, imaginative, or original things or ideas. ☐
- ☐ Doing good: contributing to the betterment of the world. ☐
- ☐ Entrepreneurship: organizing, managing, or starting a business or enterprise. ☐
- ☐ Equality: having the same capability, quantity, effect, value, or status as others. ☐
- ☐ Excitement: involvement with new and dynamic experiences with variety and change, and perhaps risk. ☐
- ☐ Fame: possessing extreme visibility or a great reputation; being recognized and renowned. ☐
- ☐ Family happiness: focusing on relationships, time spent with and attention given to children, spouse, parents, or relatives. ☐
- ☐ Financial security: pay and benefits that are satisfactory and predictable. ☐
- ☐ Friendships: frequent and caring relationships; camaraderie and interaction with others. ☐
- ☐ Fun: experiencing pleasure, amusement, and enjoyment. ☐
- ☐ Happiness: feeling or showing pleasure and satisfaction, contentment and well-being, joy or cheerfulness. ☐
- ☐ Harmony: feeling inner calm and tranquility. ☐
- ☐ Health: optimal functioning of body, mind, and spirit. ☐
- ☐ Helping others: giving assistance, support, and aid to others. ☐
- ☐ Independence: self-reliance; freedom from the influence, guidance, or control of others. ☐
- ☐ Integrity: strict personal honesty; firm adherence to a moral code. ☐
- ☐ Leadership: guiding, motivating, or directing others. ☐
- ☐ Learning: acquiring knowledge and satisfying curiosity. ☐
- ☐ Leisure: pursuing non-work-related activities. ☐
- ☐ Personal development: challenging your capabilities; acquiring new skills and demonstrating abilities. ☐
- ☐ Physical activity: involvement in activities that rely on your body and physical exertion. ☐

☐ Recognition: being positively acknowledged by others; being given special notice or attention. ☐

☐ Respect: being treated with consideration and fairness. ☐

☐ Risk-taking: facing unknown or dangerous challenges or demands. ☐

☐ Safety: freedom from danger, risk, or injury. ☐

☐ Security: protection from fear, anxiety, or danger; a guarantee of the fulfillment of an agreement; predictability. ☐

☐ Self-expression: ability to communicate personal ideas, emotions, or feelings. ☐

☐ Spirituality: participating in a religious or ecclesiastical belief system. ☐

☐ Stability: maintaining an enduring, dependable, and predictable situation. ☐

☐ Status: possessing a prestigious position or rank. ☐

☐ Teamwork: working closely with others toward common goals; having close working relationships. ☐

☐ Wealth: owning a significant quantity of money or possessions. ☐

If values that are important to you are not on the list above, write them down in the blank lines below.

☐ _____ ☐

☐ _____ ☐

☐ _____ ☐

Now that you've selected all the values that are important to you, you'll narrow down the list to your top ten values. Read through your selections on the preceding list of values, and check the box to the right of any value that you absolutely cannot or will not live without. Ask yourself, "When I've been the happiest in my life, was this value fulfilled? Is this truly *my* value, or is it an unrealistic or unauthentic ideal that I really don't live by?" If you are unable to identify ten values, that's fine. However, do try to limit your number to a maximum of ten. In the spaces below, write down your ten values in any order.

VALUE	YES	NO
1.	☐	☐
2.	☐	☐
3.	☐	☐
4.	☐	☐
5.	☐	☐
6.	☐	☐
7.	☐	☐
8.	☐	☐
9.	☐	☐
10.	☐	☐

Next, think about your current work situation. To the right of each value, check yes or no to indicate whether or not this value is being expressed in any aspect of your work right now. Whether you are pursuing a different kind of work or simply trying to change the dynamics of your current career, it is very important to know which values are most significant to you.

———————

Mary has a strong need for financial security and stability. These two values are fulfilled for her in her current job as an analyst for an investment bank. Two of her other values, however, are respect and balance, neither of which is being satisfied for her right now. Mary works with colleagues who are demanding and rude, and she consistently works sixty to seventy hours a week along with a three-hour daily commute. Mary really enjoys the kind of work she is doing and intends to look for a similar job in an industry other than investment banking. She plans on being very careful this time about assessing the culture of prospective employers to ascertain how employees work together and the ways that the company values its employees' time by supporting flextime, telecommuting, vacation, and reasonable deadlines.

By working for a company that does not support respect and balance, Mary learned the hard way about the values that are truly important to her. If Mary had known that respect and balance were so important to her, she would have asked probing questions during her interview in an attempt to understand the work environment.

You have the benefit of learning what your primary values are now so that as you move through the process of changing your work, you can keep your top ten list of values foremost in your mind. Continually refer to your list when you are analyzing and thinking about different work options.

Attitudes

Attitude is your state of mind or feelings with regard to a person, idea, or thing. Research has consistently shown that one's attitude directly motivates one's behavior. In a positive sense, those who possess an optimistic attitude about a goal or challenge are far better equipped to overcome any barriers to achieving that goal. On the other hand, an individual who has a negative attitude will find it much more difficult to achieve his or her goal. The process of assessing yourself and your work can be nerve-racking if you allow it to be. Self-assessment requires time, honesty, patience, and introspection. But even if you are willing to put in the time and effort, your overall attitude can "make or break" your ability to reach your goals.

This simple assessment focuses on your attitudes toward yourself and toward the external world as they pertain to work. For each statement, circle the word that most closely describes how you usually feel or act.

1. I have enough confidence in myself and my abilities that I am willing to take reasonable chances and do things I haven't done before in order to create satisfying work for myself.

Almost never   Seldom   Sometimes   Frequently   Almost always

2. I am uncomfortable promoting myself and think that if I'm doing a good job, the right people will notice.

Almost never   Seldom   Sometimes   Frequently   Almost always

3. I find that I really know the things I'm good at and not good at, and I think that self-evaluation is for people who are less experienced.

Not at all   Seldom   Somewhat   Frequently   Almost always

4. I feel that I put the maximum amount of time, energy, and enthusiasm into my work that I'm capable of doing.

Almost never   Seldom   Sometimes   Frequently   Almost always

5. I feel that relationships are very important to my career success and that I have developed and maintained strong relationships with people both within and outside my company and industry.

Almost never   Seldom   Sometimes   Frequently   Almost always

6. I initiate contact with my boss, my clients, and my subordinates consistently, offering support, feedback, and appreciation whenever possible.

Almost never   Seldom   Sometimes   Frequently   Almost always

7. Given the rapid pace of change and the excessive demands of employers and clients today, I don't believe that true job satisfaction is possible anymore.

Not at all   *Seldom*   *Somewhat*   *Frequently*   *Almost always*

8. When I have learned something new or make a meaningful contribution to my organization or industry, I document it immediately and then celebrate my success.

Almost never   *Seldom*   *Sometimes*   *Frequently*   *Almost always*

9. I set short-term goals for myself and include action items, which I take very seriously.

Almost never   *Seldom*   *Sometimes*   *Frequently*   *Almost always*

10. I am clear about my career goals and realize how important it is to have specific goals, monitor my own performance, and get myself back on track if I need to.

Almost never   *Seldom*   *Sometimes*   *Frequently*   *Almost always*

11. My job is so demanding that I am simply unable to get involved with professional development or keep up with reading the trade publications in my industry.

Almost never   *Seldom*   *Sometimes*   *Frequently*   *Almost always*

12. I work at keeping up-to-date on trends and other information about industries besides my own.

Almost never   *Seldom*   *Sometimes*   *Frequently*   *Almost always*

SCORE KEY

For each statement, match your answer with the numerical value listed below. For example, if you answered Seldom for statement 1, your score is 2. Then add your scores as directed.

1. *Almost never*	*Seldom*	*Sometimes*	*Frequently*	*Almost always*
1	2	3	4	5
2. *Almost never*	*Seldom*	*Sometimes*	*Frequently*	*Almost always*
5	4	3	2	1
3. *Not at all*	*Seldom*	*Somewhat*	*Frequently*	*Almost always*
5	4	3	2	1
4. *Almost never*	*Seldom*	*Sometimes*	*Frequently*	*Almost always*
1	2	3	4	5
5. *Almost never*	*Seldom*	*Sometimes*	*Frequently*	*Almost always*
1	2	3	4	5
6. *Almost never*	*Seldom*	*Sometimes*	*Frequently*	*Almost always*
1	2	3	4	5
7. *Not at all*	*Seldom*	*Somewhat*	*Frequently*	*Almost always*
5	4	3	2	1
8. *Almost never*	*Seldom*	*Sometimes*	*Frequently*	*Almost always*
1	2	3	4	5
9. *Almost never*	*Seldom*	*Sometimes*	*Frequently*	*Almost always*
1	2	3	4	5
10. *Almost never*	*Seldom*	*Sometimes*	*Frequently*	*Almost always*
1	2	3	4	5
11. *Almost never*	*Seldom*	*Sometimes*	*Frequently*	*Almost always*
5	4	3	2	1

12. *Almost never*	*Seldom*	*Sometimes*	*Frequently*	*Almost always*
1	2	3	4	5

SCORE KEY

Add the total of scores for questions 1 and 2.
_____ This is your score for Self-confidence.

Add the total of scores for questions 3 and 4.
_____ This is your score for Self-knowledge.

Add the total of scores for questions 5 and 6.
_____ This is your score for Managing Relationships.

Add the total of scores for questions 7 and 8.
_____ This is your score for Maintaining Motivation.

Add the total of scores for questions 9 and 10.
_____ This is your score for Goal Orientation.

Add the total of scores for questions 11 and 12.
_____ This is your score for Professional Commitment.

WHAT DO YOUR SCORES MEAN?

Self-confidence

If your score for self-confidence is 6 or below, you may be feeling that your work has no value or that you are not appreciated by your employer. It may be that you are not taking any risks in your work or are not feeling optimistic and open. It is more difficult to make changes when your self-confidence is not healthy. Exploring and dealing with your reasons for lower self-confidence is important. Has something happened to you in the recent past that has caused your self-confidence to erode? Can you focus on achieving something that will improve your self-confidence?

Self-knowledge

If your score is 6 or below in this category, your assessment of yourself may not be as accurate as it could be. Honestly evaluating your strengths and the areas in which you may need more development as well as asking others for feedback may be useful exercises for you to undertake. If you are unrealistic about how well you really know yourself, then you will have difficulty identifying the best possible fit for yourself in relation to work.

Managing Relationships

A score of 6 or below in this category could indicate that you don't value relationships with others or that you have concerns about your effectiveness in dealing with other people. Networking is a crucial part of learning about the external world, and without strong relationships to help you, the process of exploration can be painful.

Maintaining Motivation

If you scored 6 or below in this category, it is possible that you have neglected your career. Staying focused and energized is up to you. If you aren't consistently thinking of ways to maintain your focus and energy where your career is concerned, you will have difficulty feeling motivated. This, in turn, will make it more difficult to achieve your goals.

Goal Orientation

If your score falls below 6 here, you probably don't have a focused plan of action for achieving specific outcomes. Setting reasonable yet challenging goals and really believing in them will help you keep motivated, especially when you want to do something different with your career.

Professional Commitment

It is likely that you are bored with your work or career if you scored below 6 in this category. Think about the reasons you entered your present line of work. What about it energizes you now or did so in the past? Your answer to this question may help you regain some of your sense of commitment to your profession. On the other hand, if you have difficulty coming up with a satisfactory answer, it may make sense for you to begin the process of changing the type of work you do.

If your work situation is less than desirable, your score may be low in one or several of these categories. Don't be overly concerned! Instead, think about why this is so and what you can do about it. Any of these areas can be developed with motivation, guidance, and the right tools.

Richard has been a photographer for twenty years and has grown increasingly unhappy with the way the photography business has changed. He isn't getting enough photo shoots to pay for his studio and support his family, and he realizes that he probably will have to close his business. Unfortunately, Richard's self-confidence has eroded so badly that he feels paralyzed about pursuing another career. In addition, he thinks that because he isn't good at networking or managing relationships, he won't be successful at uncovering new job opportunities. He isn't motivated to find a job and certainly doesn't have any kind of plan in place to move forward. Richard really needs to focus on each of these areas before he can move ahead in finding new work.

Your attitude as reflected by these six categories is something to be aware of as you think about changing your work. When you are happy and satisfied with your work, your score in each area will be very high.

Change Resilience

Most people don't like change. For many of us, change can be difficult or uncomfortable. This is true regardless of whether the change is forced upon us, planned, unexpected, or self-created. Why? Because we are giving up familiarity in exchange for the unfamiliar and unknown. When this occurs, we experience a myriad of emotions, including frustration, uncertainty, and fear. *Who Moved My Cheese?* by Spencer Johnson, M.D., is a simple ninety-four-page parable offering a quick, easy, and fun way to understand change and deal with it quickly and effectively. Fear of change and what it represents is one of the reasons that people don't reevaluate their work. This assessment on change resilience is intended to help you increase your self-awareness about your comfort level with change. If you understand more clearly what your threshold of tolerance is for change, it will be easier for you to handle change and even make it happen. This is an important thing for you to know about yourself, because change is an unavoidable part of learning to find gratifying work.

When responding to the following statements, indicate how each one is true for you by placing the appropriate number in the blank to the left of the statement.

5 = *Definitely true*
4 = *Often true*
3 = *Somewhat true*
2 = *Scarcely true*
1 = *Almost never true*

_____ 1. I can honestly describe myself as someone who seeks change regularly.

2. I'm rarely surprised by changes at work because I usually see early warning signs and can prepare myself in advance.

_____ 3. I am constantly trying to learn new skills even when there is no immediate need to do so in my job.

_____ 4. When there is a change initiative going on within my company or with my clients, I am often asked by leadership to become involved in the process and implementation early on.

_____ 5. I find it easy to look at a business problem from a different standpoint even if I haven't taken this approach in the past.

____ 6. When an employee or colleague suggests another way of handling something, I encourage him or her to try it even if someone else has already tried it this way in the past.

____ 7. I work very hard at staying current in my field by belonging to professional organizations, networking with people outside my company, and keeping up-to-date with trade publications.

____ 8. I look forward with great excitement to changing my work or career.

SCORE KEY

Add up the numbers that you entered for each question. Here is what these points indicate:

8 to 19 points	You have significant difficulty dealing with change. Change is simply not comfortable for you, and you tend to avoid it at almost all costs.
20 to 29 points	Although you are able to handle change under the right circumstances, you have to be highly motivated to instigate it.
30 to 40 points	Your ability to anticipate and handle change is admirable. You are usually adept at creating and responding to change.

Anyone can learn to deal more effectively with change if there are real reasons to do so and there is a reward for changing. If you are unhappy with your work situation, instigating and accepting change is very important in order to find satisfaction in your work. This is particularly true now that there is increasing pressure for many people to make drastic changes. Whether you want to or not, this is a time when it is even more relevant for you to accept the need to change.

CHAPTER 4

Personality Preferences, Interests, and Favorite Skills

Now it's time to learn about who you are and what makes you unique, based on your individual characteristics and your personality, interests, and skills. The self-assessments in this chapter fall into three categories:

- Personality Preferences
- Interests
- Favorite Skills

Personality Preferences

Personality is the totality of an individual's distinctive traits. Although aspects of your personality can change slightly as a result of experience and self-awareness as you move through life, your inherent personality was developed by the time you were two years old. You cannot change the essence of who you are, but you *can* change your behavior. When you are looking for a good fit between who you are and the kind of work you do, it is important to know what your personality preferences are in order to ensure that they will mesh with your work.

Your personality encompasses many traits. The following statements assess some of the traits that have proved to be important when considering a career. There are no right or wrong answers when taking a personality preference test; however, it is important to respond quickly and intuitively. The statements may seem very black and white in nature, but this is intentional.

1. I like people for the most part; however, I prefer to work on my own.

Yes   *No*

2. When I enter a roomful of people I don't know, I feel shy and uncomfortable.

Yes   *No*

3. When I have to deal frequently with people on the phone or face-to-face, I feel drained by the end of the day.

Yes   *No*

4. I often think about what "could be" instead of what exists now.

Yes   *No*

5. New ideas, insights, and inferences really excite me.

Yes   *No*

6. I get bored very easily with projects that I'm working on.

Yes   *No*

7. I do not believe that it's very important to follow rules, regulations, and guidelines as closely as possible.

Yes   *No*

8. When involved in a business deal or transaction, my first concern is how the other person feels.

Yes   *No*

9. I'm more likely to be described by others as "enthusiastic and warm" rather than "calm and cool."

Yes   *No*

10. When someone at work asks me to stop what I'm doing to help with a project, I feel disjointed.

Yes   *No*

11. I love schedules, definite deadlines, and planning.

Yes   *No*

12. I like having all the information before I begin a project and become uncomfortable when priorities change.

Yes   *No*

13. When I believe in something, I am not afraid to speak up even if everyone else disagrees with me.

Yes   *No*

14. I prefer to be the leader rather than have others lead.

Yes   *No*

15. I try very hard to get people to understand my way of thinking.

Yes   *No*

SCORE KEY

Write down the number of times you answered yes for the following sets of questions:

Questions 1 to 3

_____

Questions 4 to 6

_____

Questions 7 to 9

_____

Questions 10 to 12

_____

Questions 13 to 15

_____

WHAT DO YOUR SCORES MEAN?

Introverted or Outgoing

If you answered yes more often for questions 1 to 3, you tend to be more introverted. You enjoy your solitude, don't like being the center of attention, and typically work out problems and ideas by yourself.

If more of your answers are no, you are more outgoing and prefer to be with people more often than not. You probably have many social relationships and are expressive and easy to read.

Idealist or Realist

If you answered yes more often to questions 4 to 6, you prefer to imagine possibilities and are more of an idealist. This means that you love new ideas, insights, and inferences and tend to focus your energy on the future and what could be instead of what exists now.

If you answered no more often for questions 4 to 6, your focus tends to be more on reality and less on possibilities. You take things more literally, preferring the specific and realistic rather than what you can't see or have to imagine.

Emotional or Factual

Answering yes more often to questions 7 to 9 indicates that you are more emotional than factual. Being emotional means you tend to be more focused on feelings and your personal values.

If your answers are more often no, you prefer to be factual, veering toward analysis, laws, rules, and policies.

Structure or Spontaneity

If your answers are more often yes for questions 10 to 12, you like structure and prefer planning with fixed goals that have definite deadlines.

If your answers were mostly no for questions 10 to 12, you are spontaneous and prefer goals that are more open-ended. You tend to be flexible and adaptable to changing situations.

Assertive or Acquiescent

Answering yes more often to questions 13 to 15 means your personality preference is to be assertive. This means you tend to be more dominant and more of a go-getter.

If you answered no to two or more of questions 13 to 15, you are more acquiescent, tending to have a more passive nature and preferring to be behind the scenes rather than leading the pack.

How to Use This Information

Even when you are using skills in your work that you enjoy and are interested in the work you are doing, if your personality doesn't match your work, you will not be satisfied. Kelly is an example. She is an introvert and a realist. She is emotional, acquiescent, and prefers structure. She works as a help desk professional, and while she enjoys the information technology field, Kelly goes home at night feeling exhausted by the constant barrage of phone calls and e-mails. She never seems to be able to accomplish what she sets out to do because she is constantly interrupted by requests for help from the employees of her company. Because she tends to acquiesce rather than lead, she isn't able to take control of her situation.

After you have taken the personality preference quiz, write down your preferences and compare them to your work environment to see if they fit. Let's see how Kelly's list looks:

PERSONALITY PREFERENCES	KELLY'S WORK ENVIRONMENT
Introverted	Deals with people constantly.
Realist	Kelly solves computer problems by collecting all the facts first even if it takes a long time.
Emotional	Kelly's boss and many of her colleagues focus on following rules and policies when making decisions.
Structure	There is a process that the employees of Kelly's company are supposed to follow when they need help, but this rarely happens.
Acquiescent	Kelly's passivity allows her colleagues to be demanding of her. She constantly feels pushed into a corner and often agrees to deadlines that are unrealistic because she feels uncomfortable setting limits.

Clearly, Kelly is working in a job that is not a fit for her personality preferences. Kelly would be much happier in an information technology role in which she interacts with people in a more structured way and can stick to a schedule that is self-imposed rather than forced on her.

Now you try:

_____

_____

_____

_____

_____

_____

_____

_____

_____

If you have completed your comparison of your personality preferences with your current work environment and have discovered, as Kelly has, that there isn't a strong match between the two, this could be a very good reason for your unhappiness in your work.

Interests

An interest is something that you are willing to give special attention to because you either feel strongly about the subject or you like the way it makes you feel when you are engaged with it. The degree to which you feel passionate about your interests can vary dramatically depending on your preferences with regard to the various topics or activities involved.

There are two steps to this first exercise. First, without thinking too intently, list ten activities or topics that interest you the most. They can be either work-related or non-work-related. Don't worry if you can't come up with ten.

Next, remembering your values and personality preferences, under the heading "How It Makes Me Feel" write down two or three words or phrases to the right of each interest that describe how that particular interest makes you feel or why it arouses a willingness on your part to involve yourself with it. Let me use myself as an example.

49

INTEREST	HOW IT MAKES ME FEEL
1. *Reading*	Reading allows me to escape to another place or time. I get involved with interesting characters, and I always learn something.
2. *Speaking to audiences*	Giving talks is a vehicle for expressing myself, using language, and helping people learn and understand ideas and information. Speaking provides immediate recognition.
3. *Watching movies*	The visual involvement with stories and characters makes me feel entertained and engaged.
4. *Organizing space or things*	Appeals to my need for orderliness and makes me feel in control.
5. *Socializing one-on-one*	I get energy from people, and I'm very curious about others. It feels good to laugh, tell stories, and exchange information.
6. *Walking or sitting at the beach*	The beautiful environment and the sun relax me.
7. *Eating and drinking in restaurants*	A social activity, and I love the sensations involved.
8. *Writing*	Venue for using language and helping others.
9. *Giving advice and solving problems*	I like the intellectual challenge; I can make a difference.
10. *Riding on trains*	I like this speedy and efficient way to travel, and I find it relaxing.

Now you try:

INTEREST	HOW IT MAKES ME FEEL
1.	
2.	
3.	
4.	
5.	
6.	
7.	
8.	
9.	
10.	

Determining your primary interests is usually relatively easy, especially if you regularly spend time doing things such as playing golf or making stained-glass windows. What is difficult for most people is thinking about interests in relation to work. Many people tend to separate the two because they believe that they won't be able to fulfill their interests through work. Yet the people who are the most satisfied with their careers have found a way to tie their personal interests more closely to their work. This can mean creating more time outside of work to pursue their interests or working in a field or industry that involves their interests. Here are two examples: Barry works as a sales manager in the grass seed business. A major part of his job is playing golf—a sport that Barry is passionate about—with his clients, who are owners and managers of golf courses. Candace works in human resources, but her schedule is flexible enough that she can take two to three bike trips every year.

This assessment can help you think about how to relate your strongest interests to work. For example, I am a professional speaker, a writer, a coach, and a consultant. My work satisfies my interest in speaking to audiences, writing, giving advice and solving problems, and socializing one-on-one. I have often fantasized, however, about writing restaurant or movie reviews, which would combine my interests in writing, socializing one-on-one, watching movies, and eating and drinking in restaurants. Just because I love eating in restaurants does not mean that I want to own one or work in one. In fact, I did work in restaurants and disliked it.

Can you think of ways in which you can tie your interests into work based on the examples that have been provided? What are they?

_____

_____

_____

_____

_____

The next exercise is designed to help you understand your interest in specific types of work tasks and activities. Simply check the tasks and activities that appeal to you, regardless of the level of interest you have. You may or may not have tried these tasks before. For now, ignore the letter that follows each item.

____ Scheduling tasks or meetings   (D)
____ Counseling someone   (P)
____ Chopping wood outside   (O)
____ Participating in a sports team   (P)
____ Operating machinery   (O)
____ Planting flowers or a garden   (O)

___ Learning new software   (O)
___ Keeping records   (D)
___ Preparing food   (O)
___ Taking care of someone who is ill   (P)
___ Analyzing and managing investments   (D)
___ Negotiating a deal between two parties   (P)
___ Writing a business or sales proposal   (I)
___ Conducting research   (D)
___ Revamping a compensation plan   (D)
___ Handling customer complaints   (P)
___ Going on a sales call   (P)
___ Designing an audio system   (I)
___ Word-processing a document   (D)
___ Organizing a desk   (I)
___ Teaching a class   (P)
___ Selling products in a store   (P)
___ Writing an article   (I)
___ Designing a Web site   (I)
___ Driving an eighteen-wheel truck   (O)
___ Taking care of children   (P)
___ Breeding racehorses   (O)
___ Preparing financial statements   (D)
___ Finding markets for new products   (I)
___ Interviewing a job applicant   (P)
___ Coordinating an event   (I)
___ Writing a press release   (I)
___ Repairing a watch   (O)
___ Planning a budget   (D)
___ Rewiring a house   (O)
___ Building a cabinet   (O)
___ Preparing accounting reports   (D)
___ Finding a new office space   (D)
___ Facilitating a meeting   (P)
___ Acting as a travel guide   (P)
___ Designing a costume   (I)

____ Opening new accounts for customers   (P)
____ Reviewing restaurants   (I)
____ Managing a group of employees   (P)
____ Raising money for a cause   (P)
____ Creating spreadsheets   (D)
____ Drawing maps   (O)
____ Fighting a fire   (O)
____ Analyzing census data   (D)
____ Writing a book   (I)
____ Reupholstering a couch   (O)
____ Decorating a house   (I)
____ Raising cattle   (O)
____ Designing a new business procedure   (D)
____ Conceptualizing a company vision   (I)
____ Creating a marketing campaign   (I)
____ Maintaining golf course greens   (O)
____ Writing a blog   (I)
____ Analyzing insurance risk   (D)
____ Editing manuscripts   (I)
____ Reviewing legal contracts   (D)

Each of the tasks and activities listed above falls into a specific type of interest category. The four categories are People, Ideas, Data, and Objects. Now look at the letter in parentheses next to each task or activity. Count the number of P's, I's, D's, and O's you have and write each number in the corresponding space below.

P   ____

I   ____

D   ____

O   ____

Read the definition of each interest category below. The category with the highest number is your dominant interest.

People

You enjoy activities or tasks that involve a lot of interaction with people, whether individually or in groups. You may enjoy persuading, teaching, coaching, counseling, or directing people. Regardless, the key for you in your interests is to be involved with people the majority of your work time.

Ideas

This category involves theory, concepts, and the creation or expression of feelings, philosophy, or beliefs. You probably tend to lean toward the arts, music, drawing, painting, sewing, and writing.

Data

You are most interested in concrete and realistic tasks that involve schedules, numbers, financials, directions, procedures, and processes. You appreciate and are comfortable with the finite and practical nature of tasks or activities that fall into this category.

Objects

You like working with your hands, repairing things, and the precise and orderly use of machinery, tools, and inanimate objects. Working with plants and animals are part of this category.

Most people are primarily interested in one of these categories but enjoy and want to be involved with tasks in another category as well. Bernie, for example, loves his work in technical sales, yet has a degree in engineering and really gets involved in the design and installation of the equipment he sells. He's fortunate enough to be able to satisfy his interests in two distinctly different areas.

Favorite Skills

A skill is an ability or expertise. A favorite skill is a skill that you not only possess but are also *interested in* and *willing to use*. This is the difference between a skill and a favorite skill.

Although a skill can be defined as a broad category, like verbal reasoning or spatial relations, this assessment is focused on helping you understand how to identify specific skills that you can and want to use in your work, such as writing or scheduling, for example. We all have skills that we are good at but that we are not necessarily interested in using frequently or at all. While it is unrealistic to expect that you can avoid using certain skills without exception, it is not unreasonable to expect to spend the majority of your time at work using the abilities that you enjoy and are eager to use—your favorite skills.

For each skill or competency on the following list, you will assess two things:

1. What you believe is your degree of proficiency.
2. Whether or not you enjoy using it.

For degree of proficiency, use the scale provided and write the number that applies in the space to the right of the skill. For enjoyment, check those skills or competencies you enjoy using most in the space at the left. If you come across a particular skill that you haven't used in the past but think you'd enjoy using in the future, put an asterisk in the space at the left.

DEGREE OF PROFICIENCY

    0—*Untested/never tried*
    1—*Very limited*
    2—*Below average*
    3—*Average*
    4—*Above average*
    5—*Outstanding/mastery*

ENJOY MOST   DEGREE OF EXPERTISE
____ Writing business documents   ____
____ Editing materials   ____

___ Interviewing/hiring people   ___
___ Mediating differences between people   ___
___ Mentoring others   ___
___ Negotiating deals   ___
___ Public speaking   ___
___ Facilitating a meeting   ___
___ Presenting ideas   ___
___ Coaching someone   ___
___ Counseling someone   ___
___ Teaching a class   ___
___ Motivating people   ___
___ Building a team   ___
___ Leading a team   ___
___ Training people   ___
___ Helping others   ___
___ Cataloging items   ___
___ Handling scheduling   ___
___ Keeping records   ___
___ Conducting research   ___
___ Evaluating ideas   ___
___ Taking inventory   ___
___ Setting standards   ___
___ Assessing quality   ___
___ Gathering data   ___
___ Giving advice   ___
___ Approving decisions   ___
___ Delegating tasks/responsibility   ___
___ Developing procedures   ___
___ Managing people   ___
___ Solving problems   ___
___ Managing projects   ___
___ Instigating change   ___
___ Interpreting policy   ___
___ Managing tasks   ___
___ Analyzing budgets   ___

____ Overseeing a profit-and-loss statement   ____
____ Planning a budget   ____
____ Cost accounting   ____
____ Analyzing investments   ____
____ Financial planning   ____
____ Auditing   ____
____ Developing policies   ____
____ Conceptualizing new ideas   ____
____ Developing strategy   ____
____ Selling a product or service   ____
____ Telemarketing   ____
____ Creating a marketing plan   ____
____ Writing proposals   ____
____ Setting fee schedules   ____
____ Creating an advertising campaign   ____
____ Promoting a product or service   ____
____ Coordinating events   ____
____ Analyzing markets   ____
____ Managing sales   ____
____ Fund-raising   ____
____ Serving customers   ____
____ Handling customer complaints   ____
____ Working with computers   ____
____ Designing technical products   ____
____ Building something   ____

Now, from your list above, write down the ten favorite skills that you would most enjoy incorporating in your work (not necessarily in order of preference).

1.

2.

3.

4.

5.

6.

7.

8.

9.

10.

How many of your top ten favorite skills do you use in your current job? Which ones?

_____

_____

_____

_____

How many of your strengths are above average or outstanding?

_____

_____

_____

_____

Which ones could you develop more?

_____

_____

_____

_____

Which ones haven't you tried before?

_____

_____

_____

_____

Getting to know yourself as well as you can is always an enlightening and useful process. In some instances your scores and results will merely confirm what you already know about yourself. In other cases you may be surprised by what you learn. Sometimes taking assessments will highlight ideas, assumptions, feelings, and strengths that you are aware of on some level but have not thought about in a long while or have kept submerged within your subconscious.

By going through the assessment process, you've taken an important and practical first step toward giving yourself insight into what kind of work will satisfy you. This, in turn, will help you devise an action plan and, ultimately, a solution for finding satisfying work. You will need to refer to your answers to all the self-assessments as you create action plans for your specific work situation.

Now you will move on to the chapters that describe the six categories you read about in chapter 2. Each chapter will provide you with a description of the specific situation, stories of people who fit into the category, and additional assessments that you can take to help you identify what to do next. Your challenge will be to discover what you can do to find, create, or change your current work to meet your needs. Once you have identified these things and are able to couple them with the confidence to make the adjustments that are needed, the process will be easier and more fun.

PART III

How Do You Get There?

CHAPTER 5

Where's the Meaning?

In a survey that I conducted of 110 people, more than 90 percent ranked "finding meaning" as the number one reason that they recently had changed or would like to change their careers. The concept of "finding meaning" has so many interpretations that entire books have been written on the subject. The dictionary defines meaning as something that is signified or that has intent or purpose. To find meaning in work can denote being passionate about what you do and whom you do it for, or it can simply reflect your ability to set priorities in your work to satisfy your unique needs and desires. You may already know what meaning is for you, and you may realize that it doesn't exist in your work right now. Or you may not know exactly what meaning is for you, yet you know instinctively that it doesn't exist in your current work situation.

Despite being aware of the absence of meaning in their lives, some people never feel compelled to search for it. When it comes to work, it is much easier to focus on earning a paycheck to feed, clothe, and provide shelter for yourself and your family than it is to examine your purpose and passion.

Every person is different; what is deeply meaningful to you may not matter in the least to someone else. The point is that to find meaning in your work you first must know what matters to you.

Take the case of Steve, a financial consultant who owns his own business. Steve strongly believes that we can all acquire financial security if we know how to plan our finances. He gets tremendous satisfaction every day from helping his clients learn how to handle financial challenges. Steve's top values are autonomy, family happiness, financial security, and helping others.

For Chris, a twenty-four-year-old administrative assistant at a television network, meaning comes from the knowledge that he is valued by his boss and coworkers for doing a good job. Even though the tasks he performs are essentially viewed as "grunt" work, he knows that he is needed. Chris is motivated by teamwork, recognition, respect, and learning.

Both Steve and Chris know what is meaningful to them. Based on the knowledge of what would bring a sense of meaning to his work, Steve, who had a previous career in sales, made the decision to get the necessary licenses and certifications so that he could help others manage their money. Chris knows that he won't be doing entry-level administrative work forever, and his mature attitude has enabled him to satisfy his need for meaning for the moment.

You may know what meaning is for you and realize that you don't have it, or you may not know exactly what it is but feel as if you don't have it. Nonetheless, one thing is certain: In order for you to find meaning, you need to be able to question the nature and purpose of the work you are doing now.

Step 1: Complete the "Where's the Meaning?" Self-Assessment

Before you learn how to incorporate meaning into your work, it is important to come up with your own personal definition of "meaning."

Your values are particularly important to understanding what meaning is to you. Remember that values are what fulfill you and motivate you. Go back to the list of values that you identified as most important to you on page 33 and review them.

Next, keeping your top ten values in mind, ask yourself the following questions and write down your answers:

1. When you think about the things you find meaningful, what comes to mind? Include things that are significant or important in your career as well as in your personal life. Your list of "things" should include ideals and feelings as well as activities.

   _____

   _____

   _____

   _____

   _____

2. Which of these things are you involved with now? Which have you done in the past? Which would you like to be involved with in the future? Be as specific as possible.

   Past

   _____

   _____

   _____

   _____

   Now

   _____

   _____

_____

_____

Future

_____

_____

_____

_____

3. Take another look at your answers to questions 1 and 2 and narrow down your list. Be honest. Are there things on your list that you believe are meaningful but you know deep down that you'd never really pursue?

_____

_____

_____

_____

It is very important to find out what is actually meaningful for *you*. Understand that for one person meaning may be about spending more time with her children by shortening her commute and working from home one day a week, while for another it could mean reading to the visually impaired. Also be aware that the word "meaning" can be misconstrued to represent exalted ideals. In other words, meaning does not necessarily indicate that you are helping others or working for a charity.

Do not move on in this chapter if you are not clear about what meaning is for you. It is essential to know what you are working toward as you create a plan or learn how to overcome the obstacles to bringing meaning into your work.

One more point about knowing what is meaningful for you: Whatever you identify as having meaning for you today probably wasn't what was meaningful to you ten years ago and may not be so twenty years from now. What is relevant about the process of identifying and finding your meaning is that once you learn how to do it, the next time will be that much easier.

Now read the ten types of meaning and check the ones that are most important to you. You may feel that all ten types of meaning are important to you. If so, put an asterisk by the types that rank the highest in importance to you.

1. **Rewards and challenges:** something offered in exchange for service, to provide stimulation, renewal, or motivation (for example, money, awards, appreciation, applause, etc.). ☐
2. **Interesting field or industry:** working in an area of business that holds your attention or is somehow attractive, intriguing, or stimulating (for example, working in investment banking instead of commercial banking). ☐
3. **Expressing ideals and values:** living by or communicating standards, principles, or qualities (for example, working for a company that openly supports women and minorities). ☐
4. **Contributing/making a difference:** to give, share, or participate; to change or improve (for example, implementing a program that motivates and gives incentives to employees). ☐
5. **Solving problems:** answering questions or handling situations that present difficulty, uncertainty, or complexity (for example, working as a mediator). ☐
6. **Changing your lifestyle:** alter or modify your values, priorities, relationships, etc. (for example, work from your home office in order to spend more time with your children). ☐
7. **Feeling passionate:** experience powerful emotion or appetite (for example, work for a cause that you strongly believe in). ☐
8. **Supporting a cause:** contribute time, resources, or expertise; advocate for change on behalf of the cause; promote or

advance the mission of a social or political movement or a needy or underserved population (for example, shift from a profit-making organization to a nonprofit). ☐

9. **Innovating/creating:** introduce, produce, or imagine something new or original that contributes in some way to the general good (for example, start a company that sells environmentally sound items for the home). ☐

10. **Learning:** to gain knowledge, understanding, or expertise through experience or study (for example, lead a new project in an area that you or your company hasn't been involved with previously). ☐

These ten categories will provide you with a broad foundation from which you can better identify and describe the types of meaning that are most important to you. Look back at your answers to the questions on pages 65 and 66. Which of these fit into the ten categories you just read? If, for example, one of your answers to question 1 on page 65 is "I started a new chapter of a professional association and increased the membership to 125 active members," a few of the categories of meaning that are important to you are contributing/making a difference, supporting a cause, and innovating/creating.

Analyze all your answers this way to see if the same types of meaning keep cropping up as the most significant to you. Did your answers to the questions on pages 65 and 66 align with the types of meaning you checked in the exercise on page 67 and this page as being important to you? As you move ahead in your quest for meaning in your work, refer back to the ten types of meaning and their descriptions, using them as a framework.

Judi, who is middle-aged, has had four careers. For the past twenty years she has been in sales. She has volunteered for various causes throughout her life and is often described by people who know her as a giving individual who cares about helping others. Judi loves sales, and she is very good at it. She has successfully sold telephones, real estate, marketing promotions, mortgages, and plush toys.

Despite her adjunct volunteer work and fondness for sales, Judi felt that she wanted to combine her avocation with her vocation and took a job selling assisted-living services. She felt that she finally had found her niche. She was elated at being able to combine sales with something that held meaning for her. Then an opportunity to enter the field of fund-raising for a high-quality health system surfaced, and she decided to explore it. Judi said that fund-raising combined "my love of sales with a desire to touch people's hearts. It is an incredible feeling to be able to walk through a hospital, cancer center, rehab center, hospice residence, or nursing home and know that your efforts are supporting the services being provided to patients both in compensated and uncompensated care." Although no longer in fund-raising she has remained in this health-care system and is now promoting their new health and fitness center. She said she wished that she had realized earlier how putting the meaning in her work was what she needed for professional fulfillment and that happiness in your career is not derived from the money one earns or from successfully meeting targeted sales goals.

Step 2: Explore Roadblocks and Opportunities

Now you will identify any obstacles or barriers, either real or perceived, that could become actual roadblocks to finding your meaning. These are some examples: There isn't enough learning potential. I'm too old. I don't have a degree.

List them here:

_____

_____

_____

Most of the barriers or obstacles you have written down may not actually be real but perceived. Below are some of the most common barriers that people believe would prevent them from changing their career to find more meaning.

"I'll have to take a decrease in pay."

This is the time to address the number one fear that people have about changing their career and/or industry: money! It is generally believed that if your brand of meaning involves working in the nonprofit world or if you switch to a new industry, you will have to take a significant decrease in pay. While it is common knowledge that the nonprofit world doesn't offer robust compensation packages, there is a valuable trade-off if making a difference or supporting a cause is important to you.

Bruce is an excellent example. For twenty-five years he worked for a major New York City–based bank. He admits that of those twenty-five years he felt gratified for only eight—when he moved out of the audit and banking side of the business into an organizational development and training function. Yet even during those eight good years Bruce was never comfortable in banking but was constantly feeling that "I wasn't getting what I wanted—it wasn't ever right." When he was given the opportunity to take a separation package because the bank was merging with another bank, fearful as he was, he took it. He went through outplacement and during that time did, as he called it, "a lot of housecleaning." He took a hard look at his personal values and realized that a sense of mission and making a difference was something he craved—and that it had been missing for much of his career. One day Bruce attended a luncheon and listened to a panel of people who had successfully made the switch from the profit to the nonprofit world. Immediately, Bruce felt right at home. The proverbial "lightbulb" went on, and he knew that joining a nonprofit was clearly the path he needed to take.

After consulting for very little money or on a pro bono basis with various nonprofit organizations, Bruce was offered a job as chief financial officer of a New York City domestic violence agency. A victim of domestic violence himself while growing up, Bruce has never felt better or more fulfilled in his work. He is still number crunching but is also involved with strategy and wears innumerable other hats at the agency. He is earning less money than he did at the bank and admits that his ego was a little fragile about this at first. Nevertheless, he would never change his situation for a larger salary. If Bruce wants to, he can do consulting work on the side, write articles, and do many other things to generate extra income. Overall, his work life is less stressful, which gives him extra time and energy to pursue more of his outside interests.

As for the perception that you will have to accept less money if you switch careers, this really depends on how well you package yourself and your skills when you are "selling" yourself to potential employers or clients. Nici made a switch from being a marketing executive for an agency that worked with consumer products companies to a sales management position in the design field. Her current salary is comparable to her old one because she cleverly and effectively presented her management and marketing experience to her new employer. That and her obvious love of fashion and passionate interest in design easily convinced her new employer that Nici would be a great asset to the business.

"I'm too old."

While it is easy to look at certain fields or industries and fantasize about what it would be like to work in them—becoming a musician, an airline pilot, a sommelier, or an advertising executive—

many of us stop ourselves from turning fantasy into reality by thinking of age as an obstacle. There are hundreds of stories about courageous individuals who dreamed of pursuing a career they had previously fantasized about and did it, despite being older. Even though the reality is that we live in a society which is biased against older people, the truth is that if you have the passion, drive, and courage to change your career at an advanced age, you can do it!

At the age of forty, with four children and limited previous work experience, Bernice went to law school. Her husband wasn't too thrilled about the idea at first, but Bernice was determined. While forty may not seem old to start a new career, most of Bernice's fellow law students were half her age. When she graduated from law school, Bernice worked for a law firm to gain experience and then started her own firm. Today she runs a successful law practice and has never been happier or more fulfilled. She gets deep satisfaction from making a difference in her clients' lives by fighting for their rights, whether in a real estate deal or a divorce. She thinks she is a better attorney now than she would have been had she gone to law school before or during the time she was raising a family simply because she's wiser and more mature now.

If you have written down "I'm too old" or "The corporate world discriminates against people my age," think again. These may be accurate statements if your dream is to become a pitcher for the New York Yankees or the hottest new model in Paris. There are always going to be companies and people in the world who favor youth in the workplace. But if you have the drive and have done your homework and learned about the industry you are passionate about, nothing should prevent you from becoming a part of it.

"I don't have specific industry experience."

You may believe that having little or no experience is something that can hold you back from going into a new industry. While you may not be familiar with the business you are interested in, you do have plenty of experience and skills from doing many other things.

Business is business regardless of which industry you're in. There are always clients, customers, and stakeholders. Every business has sales, marketing, finance, human resources, product/service development, and operational needs. Goals and the need to achieve results are also standard issues in the business world.

Remember the ex-banker, Bruce? While he was very interested in moving from profit to nonprofit, he didn't want to take the time to learn how to manage a nonprofit or become a fund-raiser because sales didn't interest him. Instead, he applied his accounting and finance skills to the nonprofit world. Yes, there was a slight learning curve for him, but it wasn't as dramatic as he had originally thought it would be. He was patient about finding the right nonprofit opportunity, first learning about the business while consulting and offering his services as a volunteer. When he stepped on board as CFO, he was ahead of the game from a knowledge standpoint. His employer appreciates the different perspective that Bruce brings to their operation and feels fortunate to have an ex-banker on his staff.

Learning about a new industry can be exciting and challenging, particularly if it is one that you've always thought about or leaned toward. Volunteering for a business, doing part-time consulting, or sitting on a board or advisory council are wonderfully effective ways to get an education. Every industry has trade publications and industry-specific associations that hold regular meetings and publish newsletters. The Resources guide at the end of this book can help you identify some of them. Informational interviews are an excellent way to learn about a new industry. Networking with people to get the names of professionals who work in a specific industry, and compiling the same list of questions for each person, is a great information-gathering technique. Ask such questions as "How did you get into this field?" "What credentials, skills, and experience do you believe would be helpful for someone wishing to enter this field?" "I've described my background and some of my major accomplishments to you. Which do you think are particularly transferable to your industry?" "What are the most significant problems that you and people in your field are facing today?"

When people see that you are passionate and have spent time trying to learn about their industry, they will be much more inclined to reveal opportunities and introduce you to decision-makers.

"I don't know how to find a company that will allow me to express my ideals and values."

One of the obstacles you may face is your lack of knowledge about the type of industry, company, or environment that would support your values and ideals. Because you have taken the values self-assessment, you already know whether or not those values are being supported in your current work. If you hold tight to what is important to you, you will become more skilled at finding a work situation that will meet your needs in this area.

Ed is a perfect example. A human resource professional in his late forties, Ed had worked for a series of companies that failed to support diversity. As a gay man Ed constantly felt discomfort at having to work in an environment where he couldn't openly acknowledge his sexual preference. He also knew that his employer, a major investment house, was uncomfortable with the gay and lesbian communities. Ed's key value is to have the freedom to express his sexual preference openly. For the first time in his life he approached his job search with this important personal value uppermost in his mind.

Ed ended up at a smaller firm in the PR business that openly supports gays in the workplace. How did he do it? He networked through a gay friend who is head of human resources at this firm. His friend persuaded the leadership to bring Ed on board in a higher-level human resources role than they originally thought they needed. By taking the time to find out what really matters to him and believing that it could happen, Ed landed a job that resonates with who he is as a person. Like Judi and Bruce and Bernice, he has never been happier or more fulfilled in his work.

When exploring companies or industries with an eye toward

whether or not you'll be able to fulfill your values, you must ask tough questions and be prepared to accept the answers. In Ed's situation many firms professed to support diversity, but they really didn't—at least not to Ed's satisfaction. The better the job you do at investigating a company to find out whether or not its values and practices are really in sync with your own, the more likely it is that you will discover the truth. When trying to explore these types of concerns, ask questions such as:

How would you describe the corporate culture here?

Recognition is a value that is important to me. Can you give me examples of how the company gives recognition to its employees?

If a company resists having you talk to others besides their designated interviewing team, beware.

Sean worked for ten years as a very successful attorney with a large insurance conglomerate. While there, he was involved in a complex litigation matter, a massive refinancing, a sale of a significant business, and the purchase of an HMO. These projects sustained Sean well from the standpoint of professional challenge and the ability to contribute, solve problems, and creatively collaborate with colleagues and clients. Unfortunately, his employer's values began to change noticeably, and Sean felt as if the company he worked for was no longer in alignment with his own values and belief systems. His core belief in the importance of integrity, honesty, and family values had always motivated Sean to become involved in significant pro bono work, an activity that his company had always encouraged and even made possible for him to do, but now such opportunities were becoming scarcer. Although he was presented with many additional opportunities within the organization when he expressed his discontent to senior management, he chose to leave and became vice president of community relations for a real estate development company whose values supported his own.

"I can't make a difference."

Most human beings want to feel that they are either contributing to a greater cause or are having a positive impact on people or a process. One of the most common concerns people have is that although they would like to become involved in something where they will find this kind of meaning, they don't feel they can have a significant impact either financially or from an energy or time standpoint. Experiencing boredom in your job and feeling as if there is no meaning to your work are often connected. In 2000 the *New York Times* ran an article with the headline WANTED: BORED PROFESSIONALS WHO HAVE TEACHING IN MIND. The article described a campaign that New York City had launched to recruit 250 professionals with no teaching experience to teach in the city's most troubled schools. Among the 400 people who applied were bankers, lawyers, a judge, a speechwriter, and businesspeople who, as the then school's chancellor Harold O. Levy said, "have decided the job they are doing is not spiritually satisfying."

If you are working in a job in which you don't feel as if you are really contributing or making a difference, take a look around you. What needs to be changed, improved, revitalized, or eliminated? Nothing is perfect, and there is always room for improvement or development. Make it your mission to undertake this kind of project. If the people you work with don't want this kind of help from you, then it may be time to look for a new work situation where you *can* make a difference. As Sean, the attorney who left the insurance industry, says of his new career in real estate, "I have the opportunity to combine and apply so many of my skills in the context of projects that make a real and substantial difference to communities."

You have special qualities, strengths, and skills that you enjoy using. Instead of thinking about what the world needs, reverse your thinking and identify the ways in which you can help a coworker, a group, a cause, or an organization by using your unique talents.

Janet is fifty-three and has had eight careers. She has been a teacher, an arbitrator, and a conservation technician in a museum, and she owned her own events company—to name a few. Currently, she works as the director of volunteers for a nonprofit agency for children. While doing volunteer work at the agency, she took a look around, thought about her skills and what she likes to do, and drew up a job description. She then approached the agency and convinced them that this role was needed and that she was the best candidate for it. Janet loves her job. "I work part-time," she explains. "I am continuing to build upon the experiences and skills that I brought to this position and am learning new skills at the same time. Perfect!"

"I'm not sure how I'll solve problems in an industry I've never worked in before."

Sometimes you may not be sure that you are capable of solving a problem in an area in which you have no expertise or within an industry you don't know. The plus side of trying to solve problems in a field that is new to you is that you don't possess the habits and routine behavior patterns that often obscure the vision of someone who has worked closely in a particular industry. You can add a fresh perspective.

Gail had a long career in sales management for several large companies, and although she enjoyed it, she realized that she was tired of the day-to-day tedium of managing people. She decided to strike out on her own as a consultant working with privately held businesses. Gail always got excited about solving problems, and when she started helping small businesses solve their sales problems, she really felt as if she had found her niche.

"I don't know if I can change my lifestyle."

If you're like most people who work, you probably feel as if you don't have enough time in the day to get everything done either at work or in your personal life. You may even tend to push your family to the end of your "to do" list in deference to your job and your boss. You may be exhausted, yet you just aren't sure how you can change the way you are living.

Howard was laid off in 2009 from an executive job on Wall Street. After a month of not working, he commented to his outplacement counselor how impressed he was with his wife and children. He never knew who they were "as people" during his years of working on Wall Street and couldn't imagine ever letting his relationships with his family erode again. Although fearful that he wouldn't be able to earn the same amount of money, he researched franchises and bought one that sells juice to small companies. After a year and a half he was back to his old Wall Street salary. Sure, he had to work hard to build his business, but the flexibility he now has to spend time with his family has made a world of difference.

"I don't really feel passionate about anything."

If you have never truly felt passion for anything in your work, your greatest obstacle may well be finding out what it is that will give you this feeling. While it isn't necessary to be passionate, and most people aren't all the time, those who have taken the time to uncover their passion are truly happy, excited, and satisfied, and they view work in the same light as play. In *The Passion Plan*, Richard Chang outlines a seven-step model for bringing passion into your life. He describes passion as either content-based or context-based. Examples of content-based passion are activities such as golf, fishing, computers, and cooking, while context-based passions are centered on themes such as improvement, leadership, entrepreneurship, or competition. We can experience both types of passion in our work and in other areas.

While there may be something that you feel passionate about, if it is a hobby or an extracurricular activity, you probably think that it can't be woven into your work life. If you are a golfer, it is unrealistic to think that you can give up your day job and join the PGA tour! Yet you may be able to bring your passion for golf into your work. Frank, for example, works for a real estate management company. He manages buildings all over the United States and plays golf with half a dozen of the building managers. He has been able to combine earning a nice living with playing golf with his clients as often as he likes.

Think about what you feel passionate about. Is it something you are involved with outside of work? Is it something that you haven't been involved with in a long time? Is it something that you do at work but not enough to keep those passionate feelings ignited? Sit down with a piece of paper and write down all the ways that you can incorporate your passion into your work— forgetting for the moment any limitations that you may perceive. Or gather a small group of friends together and have a brainstorming session to generate ideas about how you can integrate passion into your work.

Not sure what your passion is? Start looking at the world through different eyes. What interests you that you've never done before? Is there an activity or hobby that you have always been drawn to but never tried? Why not find someone who does it and ask him or her to show you the ropes? Take a class or a workshop to see if it really turns you on. Whether you are interested in archery or running your own business, the only way to discover your passion is to try it!

Don waited until he retired to pursue his passion, which is teaching math to high school kids at a private school. He worked in corporate America for years and then sold insurance before "retiring" to teach math. "Yes! I am satisfied with my work," he says. "I wake up each morning looking forward to going to school. The students are challenging and fun to be with, and I love my subject."

"I don't have enough time."

In a survey of doctors, lawyers, engineers, and other high-profile executives conducted by umbershoot.net, 94 percent of those surveyed said that their dream was to help mankind. While many of us fantasize about doing good and helping the less fortunate, we may also be thinking that there's not enough time to do so. Another survey conducted by a nonprofit consortium showed that 52 percent of the United States population volunteers in community service for an average of five hours a week. If you increasingly feel the need to add meaning to your life by supporting a cause but also feel that you just don't have enough time to give, here are some suggestions.

To match your interests and skills with an organization in need of what you can offer, try looking at these Web sites: volunteermatch .org and 1-800-Volunteer.org. The Resources guide at the back of this book also lists nonprofit and charity organizations that you can contact. If you are interested in supporting a cause and earning a living doing it, consider volunteer work first so that you can get a feeling for the way nonprofit organizations operate.

Of course, finding the time to volunteer is a real problem for people who work full-time. If you are someone who needs a more structured schedule, then commit to doing something at the same time every other week. If you prefer spontaneity, then volunteer for an organization that doesn't need you to be there consistently at the same place and the same time but is more interested in whatever effort or creative contribution you can provide. Start small, offering your time and talents in limited doses. If you work for an employer who supports programs in the community, get involved through this avenue first. Or approach your company and ask them to sponsor you in a volunteer effort by giving you flexible hours or time off.

Bill was an engineer for fifteen years, and although he liked tinkering and was good at testing, he really didn't enjoy his work. He left engineering and moved into information services and general management in the telecommunications field. After five years he was laid off and took the summer to reflect on what he wanted to do. He and his wife, Mary, had volunteered part-time for many years, and Mary's career was already in the nonprofit sector. After a serious discussion with his wife, Bill decided to volunteer for a number of community organizations. Today he works as a volunteer ambulance attendant, a volunteer fireman, and a volunteer for a food collection organization. He sits on the board of an agency that donates clothing and food to low-income families, works for a food bank, and is the chairperson of his church's Christmas tree sale. In addition, he loves to sing and is a member of a choral society and a male a cappella group. He generates income from three of these activities and says, "I'm fifty-six, and it seems that a lot of people I know are doing things that aren't making them happy. We, on the other hand, are having a lot of fun!"

"I'm not very creative."

As adults we can sometimes be apprehensive or feel insecure about our ability to be creative. We convince ourselves that creativity is only for children. But with technology taking over so many of our left-brain tasks, we have more of an opportunity to create and innovate. Unfortunately, we can get so mired in day-to-day tasks and deadlines that we don't make creativity a priority. We tell ourselves it's something that we will do when we "retire" or when we go on vacation.

Creativity takes so many forms—it's not just sculpting, painting, or writing. Julia Cameron wrote a wonderful book called *The Artist's Way* in which she presents a step-by-step method for discovering and recovering your creative self. Cameron talks about taking your creative potential seriously by stopping negative talk such as "It's too late," "My friends and family will think I'm crazy," or "Creativity is a luxury, and I should be grateful for what I have." Although she wrote the book for aspiring and working artists, it is one that anyone can read to unleash the creative spirit lying dormant in all of us.

Creativity means being innovative, original, or imaginative. In the context of your current job, is there a way that you can focus more on these kinds of activities and less on the routine "business as usual" tasks? Do you have one idea that you've been thinking about for years but that you've never had the courage or taken the time to pursue?

Angie is a mid-level human resources professional at a nonprofit organization. While she fulfills her need for meaning, making a contribution, expressing her values, and supporting a cause very successfully in her job, she is constantly thinking of and inventing new products unrelated to her work. She has explored getting patents and manufacturing several of her innovations but always stops short of following through because of time, money, or family obligations. The next step for Angie should be to identify one invention and put a plan together to get a patent, find financing for manufacturing a demo of the product, and create a marketing plan. She can approach the Service Corps of Retired Executives (www .score.com), a nonprofit organization of retired executives who provide coaching to entrepreneurs. They can help her with the process so she doesn't have to pay someone for advice. Until Angie does these things, she will feel frustrated and unfulfilled despite the satisfaction she derives from her job.

Becoming the next Mozart, Rembrandt, or Shakespeare isn't what drives most people who seek to express themselves creatively, although feeling that you don't have the kind of talent those famous artists possessed may be impeding you. If you need to be more creative and innovative, the form or venue is irrelevant. What is relevant is the fact that you yearn to be more creative, and you should not wait until you have "the time or money" to do so.

"I'm not technologically savvy."
This is a statement that baby boomers in particular are guilty of repeating aloud over and over again. While it is true that Gen Xers and Millennials were born in the Internet era and have used technology throughout their formative years, this doesn't mean that those of you who weren't can't embrace, accept, or simply learn how to use technology.

Instead of viewing technology as a gigantic force you have to overcome, it is easier to look at it in small pieces. Do you want to type documents more often rather than handwrite them? Would it be easier to access and edit your calendar at the drop of a hat rather than carry around a cumbersome book? How about finding out what your doctor meant when he diagnosed your pesky health problem with a term you can't pronounce? Even if you can't spell it, just type it into your Internet browser, and it will figure it out for you.

An employer's expectation of employees' technological knowledge is that they possess a basic competence in a handful of software programs, such as Excel, PowerPoint, or Outlook, all of which have been designed intuitively for the average user. While taking a class or reading a manual or one of the *For Dummies* books is helpful, every software program becomes easier to learn when you use it more frequently. Also, it is amazing how many hundreds of resources are available to ask questions and fix technology problems.

Technology doesn't have to be used only for work; it can be used for fun, too, and sometimes this is a simpler way to learn various types of technology. David, who worked in the insurance field, never used a computer until he retired at seventy. Now eighty-four, he keeps in touch with friends and family via e-mail and plays poker on the Internet.

Step 3: Create an Action Plan

Now it's time to fill out a simple action plan to help you in your search for meaning in your work. Here is Angie's plan to use as an example:

The kind of meaning I want to pursue is . . .
Innovating/creating: I'd like to sell my thermal lunch bag in catalogs and discount stores.

The short-term action steps (tasks/activities)
I will take are . . .
1. Contact the office of patents to learn about the process for securing a patent for my lunch bag.

When will I get this done? By November 15.

2. Contact the Service Corps of Retired Executives (SCORE) to find a counselor who can help me with my business plan for launching my lunch bag.

When will I get this done? By November 30.

3. Go through the steps of applying for a patent for my lunch bag, filling out all the necessary paperwork and sending it in.

When will I get this done? By January 31.

4. With the help of my SCORE adviser, write a business plan.

When will I get this done? By February 28.

Now fill out your action plan. Although it may change based on the research you do or information you need, by putting your short-term goals on paper you will feel more committed to doing what you have to do in order to create the meaning you are yearning for in your work.

ACTION PLAN

The meaning I want to pursue is this:

_____

_____

_____

_____

_____

The short-term action steps (tasks/activities) I will take are these:

1. _____

_____

_____

_____

When will I get this done?_____

2. _____

_____

_____

When will I get this done?_____

3. _____

_____

_____

_____

When will I get this done?_____

4. _____

_____

_____

_____

When will I get this done?_____

Meaning is different for each of us. Without meaning in your work, whether it is one of the ten categories in this chapter or something that you've identified that isn't on the list, the only thing keeping you from finding it and making it happen is you. Whether it is a question of time, money, talent, attitude, drive, technical ability, knowledge, or interest—or your perception that any or all of these things can't or don't exist—there are plenty of resources to help you overcome your obstacles. Think about the kinds of meaning that are missing for you right now and start small by exploring how to add meaning to your work. Identify one thing that you can do, whether it's doing something creative, volunteering your time, researching an industry that you find interesting, or solving a problem that has been plaguing you at work. The joy and satisfaction awaiting you are indescribable.

CHAPTER 6

Been There, Done That, but Still Need to Earn

Tom is a vice president of human resources for a health-care contract research firm. At fifty-three he has made seven job changes since graduating from college, all within the human resources field. While he enjoys a large degree of independence, professional challenge, and satisfaction, he says, "I'd like the challenge of a new career. The reality is, however, that I am at a level both professionally and financially that is difficult to give up. That and the age of my children will likely keep me from pursuing an alternative career for another ten years." Additionally, Tom's savings have been annihilated in the stock market decline of 2008.

If you are like Tom, this chapter is for you. You are enjoying a successful career but can't imagine continuing to do the kind of work that you've been doing for a long time. But—and there is a big "but" here—you really need to continue earning the same amount of money or more for a given period of time or even indefinitely.

Many people in the workforce feel the way Tom does. If you are one of them, take a leap of faith and buy into the philosophy that hope and possibilities exist *if* you uncover your true interests and are willing to begin to plan the next phase of your work. Yes, there is a next phase, but only if you believe there is and are willing to do whatever it takes to make it happen. If not, you will continue to sit in your job feeling stale and trapped.

Step 1: Complete the "Been There, Done That, but Still Need to Earn" Self-Assessment

First, make an action plan folder labeled "The Work I'm Going to Do Next" and keep it somewhere within reach—not stashed away in a drawer in your desk! You'll need it to be easily accessible so that you can refer to it later.

Go back and look at the results of all the self-assessments you took in chapters 3 and 4. Begin by reviewing the values self-assessment on pages 30–33.

Now do the same with the attitudes self-assessment on pages 35–40. Are there one or two areas that you can work on within this self-assessment? Review the six categories within the attitude self-assessment. On the lines provided below, write down what you think you can do to improve your attitude in each category, keeping in mind the values that are important to you. I've made some suggestions to help you get started. Being proactive about shifting your attitude will help you jump-start the process of moving out of your Been There, Done That, but Still Need to Earn situation.

Self-confidence

In what ways can you improve your self-confidence?

Suggestion: Focus on one skill, such as networking, and practice it. Identify three new people you can meet. Call them and schedule a face-to-face meeting.

_____

_____

_____

_____

Self-knowledge
How can you improve your self-knowledge?

Suggestion: Ask three people who know you from different aspects of your life for feedback about something specific, such as the way you present yourself.

_____

_____

_____

_____

Managing Relationships
In what ways can you better manage your relationships?

Suggestion: Talk to a client, a friend, and your child or spouse about your relationships and what they'd like to get from them that may not exist now.

_____

_____

_____

_____

Maintaining Motivation
How can you better maintain your motivation?

Suggestion: Set a reasonable goal for yourself for something that you need to change or improve, such as time management or organization. Put a simple plan together with a time line for completing your plan. Document your progress.

_____

_____

_____

_____

Goal Orientation

How can you make yourself more goal-oriented?

Suggestion: Set one simple goal, such as finishing this book or writing in a journal every day for a week.

_____

_____

_____

Professional Commitment

In what ways can you deepen your professional commitment?

Suggestion: Read two trade publications (which are probably sitting in your office somewhere) in the next five days. Share one piece of information with someone else in your company or field.

_____

_____

_____

_____

Now review your results for the rest of the self-assessments you took, including your personality preferences, your score on the change resilience quiz, what your primary interests are, and your favorite skills.

Write down any and all titles, jobs, types of work, names of companies, and industries where you think you could possibly fulfill your values, top interests, personality preferences, and favorite skills. Use brainstorming techniques to do this: Write down as many ideas as come to your mind, whether they seem realistic or not. Try not to allow biases, prejudices, perceptions, or even concrete obstacles to negatively color your brainstorming process. Keep writing down words and phrases until you have run out of ideas. List them one by one on each line.

For example, Leslie wrote, "Disney, MTV, Christie's (auction house), Amazon.com, museums, interior decorator, my own business, author, architect, nonprofit, teach kids art, botanical gardens, travel writer, chef."

_____

_____

_____

_____

_____

_____

_____

_____

_____

_____

Now you are going to prioritize your thoughts and ideas based on *your level of interest*.

1. Rank every single word or phrase that you've written by placing a large number next to it on the left side, starting with number 1. Once again, don't think about your prejudices, lack of knowledge, or negative perceptions while you are prioritizing. Go with your gut. Don't spend too much time thinking about this exercise—just do it.

2. Do the same thing again, only this time write the number on the right side. Rank your words and phrases based on *how realistic it is that you can make this idea happen* (with the number 1 representing the most realistic).

In the second exercise, do not think about realism in the context of the present. Frame it in terms of "someday." By doing this you will avoid assessing the "realism" factor in terms of your ability to meet your current personal expenses. On the other hand, the amount of money you have to spend to make your goal happen *is* part of the realism factor. Let's say, for example, you wrote down "Buy a seat on the New York Stock Exchange." In 2009 a seat on the New York Exchange sold for between $500,000 and $1,000,000, and there are only 1,366 seats, mostly unavailable. Therefore, while your interest level may be high, your realism ranking is not because of the high cost of entry and the limited availability of seats.

When you finish these exercises, review your lists carefully and look for any surprises or common themes. What are they? Do the job titles, industries, and work you prioritized as your top five

interests match any of the five that led the list when you prioritized them from a reality perspective?

Now look at your list of top values, interests, and motivated
abilities from the assessment you took and compare it to your top
five job, industry, or work interests. Based on the knowledge you
have, will these things provide you with what you want and need?
We'll come back to this later in the chapter.

Step 2: Explore Roadblocks and Opportunities

Having a career plan in place—with practical, achievable goals—
significantly increases the probability of realizing those goals.
Otherwise, you might sit and stagnate for another two or three
years.

Let's explore the financial aspects of your situation. As popular
financial-planning guru Suze Orman says in her best-selling book
The Nine Steps to Financial Freedom, "It is never too soon to begin,
and it is never too late to start." If you are dealing with exorbitant
expenses, undoubtedly this is creating stress for you and your family. Revisiting your finances to learn where you can make sensible
changes can only help to relieve this stress.

Start by making an appointment with a financial planner. Be
sure to find one through a referral from someone whose judgment
you trust. Also be sure to choose someone who is truly skilled at
putting a plan together for you and is not just interested in selling
stocks or mutual funds. Be prepared to fill out a "Net Cash Flow
Form" that shows your monthly expenses and income. A good financial planner will also help you understand your net worth and
comprehend your tax situation more clearly. While you may have
met with a financial planner before or have investments for which
you receive advice, it is unlikely that you have ever *tied financial
planning into your career* before. Most people tend to keep these two
very important aspects of their lives separate until something happens, such as the sudden loss of a job. You need to know which of
your assets and financial investments you will be able to use in

order to finance a new venture, such as starting a business or changing careers.

If the top five jobs or industries you elicited from your brainstorming session are not at all related to your current job, then you probably aren't assured of being able to earn at your current level. In fact, most people automatically assume that if they switch fields or start a business, they will have to accept a drastic cut in pay. This doesn't always turn out to be true, however, but whether it's true or not, knowing you will disappoint yourself if you don't make a career change at some point, it's time for you to become familiar with your expenses, cash flow, and entire financial picture so that you can plan accordingly.

Some expenses, such as college tuition and alimony payments, are fixed for a definite period of time. Others, such as special education and treatment for a disability and an elderly parent in an assisted-living residence, are more difficult to plug into a time frame. Regardless of the categories that your expenses fall into, you should tell your financial planner that you intend to change careers. He or she will help you set financial goals aligned with your needs so that you can make a financially sound change.

Remember Tom, the human resources executive who believed that being financially responsible for his children would prevent him from pursuing a new career for another ten years? In ten years Tom will be sixty-three, and while many people are still vibrant and interested in learning new things at that age, Tom's energy and his career interests will be dramatically different by then.

If you are like Tom, what should you do? In addition to completing the assessment at the opening of the chapter and consulting with a financial planner, you should also examine the less tangible aspects of money. What are your attitudes toward it? How important is earning a good salary to you, beyond your financial responsibility to your family? Author Suze Orman hones in on these "softer" aspects of dealing with money, helping readers become aware of how they were raised to think about dealing with money and what is at the root of their specific financial habits, such as spending and saving.

If you haven't already done so, review the options available to you for reconfiguring your present job. Go through the exercise of writing down every one of the jobs you have held since college and identify three things:

1. Your level of satisfaction in the role and the reasons for it (whether you were satisfied or not).
2. Your greatest one or two accomplishments while in each position.
3. The strengths and skills you learned and used to achieve these accomplishments.

Once you have identified these things, you will see some consistent themes for what makes you feel happy and satisfied in your work, and what does not. Write down these themes and then look at your current position and think about ways you can increase the factors that bring you job satisfaction or how to find them without changing jobs.

You should also do what many people do: Look at ways to fulfill your interests outside your job. Eventually, an outside interest or activity can turn into a full-time job — with pay!

Sue is a good example of this. For seven years she has worked as a public relations coordinator for a nonprofit organization. When she had been in her full-time position for about three years, she started her own public relations business on the side and accumulated fifty or so clients with whom she works at different times. Sue is a widow and wants to feel more financially comfortable before launching her own business on a full-time basis, which is her goal. While Sue does not quite fall into the Been There, Done That category, she is a good example of someone who has cautiously planned her next career because of her need to earn enough money. She also falls into the Yearning to Be on Your Own category, and by building her business on a part-time basis while earning a regular paycheck, she is satisfying this need as well.

Most people can use the counsel of an outside expert to help them make tough but meaningful changes in their lives. At forty-three, Alison has worked in the publishing industry her entire career. Not only does she feel worn out from working in the same field for so long, but she also admits that she never has been happy in publishing.

"Although I like business, I'm not really the corporate type," Alison says. "I like to learn about what makes people tick. I don't care about fifteen-million-dollar annual quotas. I focus too much stress and energy on a large entity that does not acknowledge me as a person or recognize my talents as an individual . . . such as my communication skills, sense of humor, and holistic approach to doing business.

"I want to start my own thing," she explains, "but am so multi-faceted that I don't know how to create one thing, and I don't have the cash to create it. But I'm not giving up!"

What Alison needs to do is focus on some viable career options and develop a financial plan, which will help her overcome the obstacle of not having enough money.

Step 3: Create an Action Plan

Now it's time for you to create a plan with concrete steps that will move you out of your Been There, Done That mode.

Your plan should answer the following questions:

• What are all the career or work paths that interest you and are realistic? While the realism factor may not be obvious if you haven't yet investigated what is required to enter a specific field, you'll still be able to make some guesses about this. You can narrow your list later once you've gathered more information. For now you may want to focus on the list of jobs and industries you prioritized earlier in this chapter.

• What kind of research must you do to learn more about what is entailed in the work you've deemed interesting? To find the answers to this question, you might network at trade association meetings, set up informational meetings with people who work in the job or industry you're interested in, go on interviews, search the Internet, or visit the reference section of the library. While researching the quantifiable aspects of work, such as salaries and educational requirements, is important, the best information comes from talking to people who do the kind of work you think you want to do. Create a list of questions that you can ask everyone you meet so that you will be prepared and will remember everything you heard. Having a list will also help you compare the answers you hear to form your own conclusions. Here are some questions you can ask:

How did you get into this field?

What experience or characteristics do you think I'm lacking?

What are my advantages?

What suggestions do you have for identifying job opportunities?

• What is a pragmatic time line for moving into another career? Many of your decisions about this will depend on the plan that you and your financial planner create. Without a plan you won't be able to be specific about your time frame for achieving your career goals. Make sure to factor in the time it will take to prepare for and launch your new career. Depending on your situation, this will include such things as getting a degree or certification, finding real estate space, conducting a job search, and the legal processes involved with transactions like buying a franchise or a business. Any of these can take six months to a year to accomplish. If you have decided that you absolutely cannot change careers for, say, another four years (perhaps you're not really being realistic), you should still put an action plan in place to help you deal with your Been There, Done That symptoms. Your plan may include learning new skills, working toward a new role within your company or industry, or improving your competence in an outside hobby.

Here are some additional steps to creating an effective action plan:

• Create criteria for yourself that will help you decide when and why you might stop exploring a specific career path. Angela sold shoes from the time she graduated from college. When she was thirty-eight, she started to question how fulfilled she was at her job and "wondered if I could continue to sell shoes to retail stores between Washington and Boston for the next twenty-two years. But what else could I do? My family depends on me to provide 40 percent of the income needed to keep our lifestyle going. I explored becoming a teacher, but the study period was too long, and there wasn't enough money in it. I also explored opening my own business as a Kindermusik or Music Together franchisee, but there was already a lot of competition for children's activities in my geographic area, and they could not give me a franchise in the areas I wanted. I looked into opening my own not-for-profit corporation to help educate and empower the needy but decided I would be too much at the mercy of private and public foundations." Although the results were disappointing for Angela, because she had spent time assessing her own needs and desires carefully, it was easier for her to walk away from a possible career option as soon as it became clear that it would not meet her criteria.

• Create a realistic time line for each of the goals in your plan. Since you aren't trying to make a career change tomorrow, don't try to do too much at once or you will feel overwhelmed and probably give up on your search. Perhaps doing one research activity every two weeks would be good for you. On the other hand, since you don't have an immediate sense of urgency, it's very important to set goals to keep you on track, using your goals and deadlines as motivation to keep you going.

• Find someone to confide in and share what you are doing. Ask this person to be your informal coach and to check in with you periodically to find out how you're doing with your plan so that you'll feel accountable to someone other than yourself.

• Keep an open mind to possibilities that may not have occurred to you. Despite all her exploration, Angela, the persistent shoe salesperson, didn't feel any closer to identifying a new career until a client of hers who owned a shoe store passed away suddenly at forty-two. Her client had not planned for a premature death, and his shoe store was the only source of income for his family. His wife did not know how to run the business on her own, so their son quit college to run the store to support the family. Her late client's misfortune was an eye-opener for Angela. "I couldn't believe how a lack of planning could effectively disrupt an entire family's hopes and dreams for the future so thoroughly," she recalls. It was then that Angela realized she could use her desire to help and teach others by pursuing an occupation that could be both personally and financially rewarding. She became a financial representative for an insurance and financial company—a career path that had never before occurred to her.

• Start scheduling networking and informational meetings to gather information and meet people. In chapter 12 you will learn specific tips on how to network. Networking is one of the most useful business skills you can develop. Start your networking process with people with whom you feel most comfortable. If you don't know anyone in the jobs or fields that interest you, you'll have to find them first. Do this by making a list of ten or fifteen people whom you trust and who seem well connected to diverse groups of people. It doesn't matter what the people you network with do for a living; what matters is whom they know. Everyone knows someone.

• When you are gathering information about a field or industry, don't speak to just one person who works in the area you've targeted. Ask all those you meet with for the names of two people in their industry whom you might call or e-mail. Meet with half a dozen people who have varying levels of experience (not just senior-level people) so that you can see the complete picture. Ask such questions as the following:

What do you enjoy about your job and your industry?

What do you dislike?

What are the three things you'd recommend I do to get into your field?

What are the dominant skills that you use most frequently in your job?

Who are the players in your industry that I should meet?

Nick was unemployed. Although he had worked in technical support in the telecommunications industry, he had always had a strong interest in real estate and even had some experience managing family property. He decided to investigate what he needed to do to become a property manager in commercial real estate. He started networking to find people in that field with whom he could talk. He set up his first informational meeting with a real estate broker. During their conversation, the broker made the offhand comment that property managers are all in their late twenties and early thirties. Nick, forty-nine, was gripped by a feeling of insecurity when he heard this and immediately stopped networking. Based on one offhand remark, Nick decided that he would never get a job as a real estate property manager because he was too old. If Nick had continued networking, he might have learned that this simply wasn't so—and even if it were, he might eventually meet or be referred to someone who would be in a position to help him pursue his dream. Although your networking should be targeted, you also need lots of people so you can hit the jackpot with the right job opportunity.

Keep a file or notebook exclusively for all the information and names you gather, or you can create a contact list on your computer with the names of those with whom you are networking and notes about your meetings with these new people.

While you are networking with people and gathering information about industries that interest you, be very inquisitive about the future trends that are taking place within those industries. The World Future Society (www.wfs.org) publishes a magazine about trends in the future called *The Futurist*, which covers work, business, and industry trends. If you are not planning to move into your new career for several years, it is important to be aware of the ways that things could change, either positively or negatively.

Once you have gathered enough information to know whether or not it is realistic for you to plan on moving into a particular career, here are some things you can and should do to maintain your interest in your potential new career and accelerate your success once you actually do make your move:

• Is a specific degree or certification needed or strongly recommended for your new career? If there is, can you begin studying now on a part-time basis?

• Are there skills you will need to strengthen or have never used that you can begin to work on now? If your plan is to open your own business, for example, and you don't have a clue about accounting or sales, why not take some classes at your local college or university?

• Can you arrange to work part-time at night or on weekends in the field you are interested in, either in a barter situation or for a nominal amount of money, so that you can learn?

• During your networking process, have you met someone who would be a good mentor or coach for you? Many people are flattered to be asked to be a mentor, especially if their investment of time won't be too significant. This is a great way to start learning about a new business.

You may not be able to eliminate or even diminish your financial obligations right now, but you are still in control of planning for your future and, most important, of ending your Been There, Done That blues.

CHAPTER 7

Bruised and Gun-shy

It will come as no great revelation to you that working is difficult. Whether you have always worked for large corporations or for a mix of small and medium-sized privately held companies, you probably have a horror story to tell about a specific job situation. If you have been laid off, discriminated against, or had to deal with a psychotic boss, you are affected adversely both while you're involved in the situation and after you leave, whether you realize it or not. Not only can your negative experience color your outlook about new work opportunities, but it can also prevent you from moving forward in your job search or career when you really need to. This is especially relevant today as scores of people have lost their jobs and are struggling to find employment. Many people who have been fortunate enough to find another job are accepting lower salaries and titles, commuting long distances, or engaging in work that they did in the beginning of their careers. Many survivors of layoffs are feeling abused and unrecognized. Pauline works at a major financial services company where nearly every employee over sixty has been laid off, and the younger employees remaining are expected to work twelve-hour days without additional compensation or time off.

In her book *Are You a Corporate Refugee?*—which she calls "a survival guide for downsized, disillusioned, and displaced workers"—psychotherapist Ruth Luban tells dozens of stories about individuals who have been "innocent victims of business forces beyond their control." The book is packed with tips, resources, and suggestions for healing and moving through specific "recovery stages" to an eventual period of renewal and new beginnings.

While it is extremely important to deal with what has happened to you and put it into perspective, it is equally important to move on, to identify and engage in a type of work situation that is best for you. This chapter is for you if you're a "corporate refugee": You need to recover, and you need to work.

Melody is an insurance underwriter who retired early, presumably to keep her husband company because he had already retired. She admitted later that after taking two years off "to retire," the real reason she dropped out of the workforce is that she "felt beaten." "The worst thing for me was the eighteen months I spent in the job I had," Melody explains. "It truly was an environment where I felt personally attacked. I never should have stayed. I would not have stood for that abuse at age thirty or forty, but I let it happen at forty-eight or fifty. I lost all my confidence at that job. So two years ago, at fifty-three, I restarted. If this new job doesn't turn out as promised, I won't stay this time. I expect to be treated as well as I treat people, and I want the money."

It is not surprising to discover that people aren't very comfortable admitting that they feel Bruised and Gun-shy. Perhaps they feel it isn't professionally appropriate to admit that a negative experience has affected them adversely or that they might be viewed as "damaged goods." Whatever someone's reasons are for not admitting that they were defeated by their specific work experience, the fact remains that at one point or another it happens to most of us. The important thing is to be able to deal with your emotions and feelings about what happened to you. Until you do this effectively, it will be tough to move on.

Suzanne, an administrator in the nonprofit sector, was terminated—unfairly, she thought—because she did not have a master's degree, and the executive director said she needed one. She was upset not only because she loved her job but also because she felt she excelled at it. She also thought that age discrimination was at play in the executive director's decision to fire her. It took more than a year for Suzanne to recover. Her assessment of the workplace today? "It is complicated, to say the least! We have a workforce where mediocrity is the rule. Loyalty is practically non-existent. Moreover, youth means everything even though experience may be lacking. Workers over the age of forty-five are not desirable, nor, in many cases, are they respected by coworkers and managers. Things are not changing on that front in spite of what's being said by the media. I and others I've met have personally experienced situations where concern about upsetting the chemistry of a team is of the greatest concern—not what you know or how you may help—especially when the team members are between twenty-five and thirty-four. I'm fifty-five—need I say more?"

While age discrimination was Suzanne's issue, feeling Bruised and Gun-shy can happen at any age or time in your career. Jillian was laid off from her first job out of college at a television station because her boss, the director of research, was forced into early retirement. So Jillian's position as her assistant also became extinct. She was then fired from her next job at a radio station because her computer skills weren't up to snuff. At the tender age of twenty-three, Jillian was Bruised and Gun-shy. Her college degree was in broadcasting, and it had never occurred to her that she would do anything else for a living. The thought of finding yet another job in a field where Jillian felt she was "not a very good fit" was not appealing. Her next job after the radio station was as a contingency recruiter for an employment agency. It was the beginning of a long and happy career in sales for Jillian.

Resources and support are important—and available—to help you deal with your emotional state about your painful work situation. Seeing a counselor or therapist can help you understand and sort out your emotions much more quickly than trying to do it on your own.

Bruised and Gun-shy

Suzanne, now happily employed as a copy editor for a small publishing company where she is using many of the skills she used in nonprofit, also has some sage advice for others that she followed successfully herself: "Don't be too hard on yourself. Give yourself time to heal and don't carry the experience around with you. Move on! Spend some time being good to yourself. Getting terminated from a job happens to others every day, and it has not been known to kill anyone yet." She adds, "Remember, it's not always about you! Sometimes it's about your manager or something completely nonsensical that has nothing to do with the quality of your work or reality! And if you feel as if you have been illegally dismissed or discriminated against, contact the Department of Labor for advice." The Department of Labor, which has a division that deals with these issues specifically, will answer your questions and determine whether intervention is an appropriate next step. They will also write letters on your behalf.

Ruth Luban has some additional recommendations for those who are Bruised and Gun-shy and having difficulty moving beyond this stage. She stresses the importance of working through the five stages she describes in her book:

1. **On the Brink:** When you know something is wrong and that you may soon be a "refugee."
2. **Letting Go:** When you leave your work situation and begin to grieve.
3. **In the Wilderness:** When you are "living in ambiguity and allowing for this period of time of not knowing."
4. **Seeing the Beacon:** You have ideas, experiment with things, and start to "see the light."
5. **In the New Land:** You have found firm footing and are beginning a new cycle of renewal in a new work situation.

Understanding and moving through these five cycles will help you normalize the emotional experience of being Bruised and Gun-shy.

Step 1: Complete the "Bruised and Gun-shy" Self-Assessments

A recurring theme and recommended first step in this book is to know yourself first before you reach out to the external world. If you know your preferences, your values, and your parameters, you will find it easier to understand your needs and boundaries in a work situation. For example, if stability, security, affiliation, and a regular paycheck are important to you, starting a business or working as a free agent may not be the best choices for you to pursue. First, review the results of the values, attitudes, and change resilience self-assessments you completed earlier in chapter 3, on pages 33, 37–38, and 41–42. By doing this you will have a better chance of identifying the best job for you and avoiding another unpleasant work situation.

It makes sense to reflect on your past work situation to help you assess what you'll need and want in your future work. Using the results of the self-assessments you just reviewed, think about the specific work situation that was difficult or painful for you and answer the following questions.

VALUES

Were my values truly being met in that particular work situation?

_____

_____

Which ones were?

_____

_____

_____

Which values were not?

_____

_____

_____

ATTITUDES

Look back at the job or work situation that caused you to feel Bruised and Gun-shy and assess what you have learned about your attitudes.

_____

_____

_____

_____

_____

SELF-CONFIDENCE

Has your self-confidence eroded? If it has, focus on using one of your strengths or skills to help regain your confidence.

If you are working now, is there a task or project you can complete or a goal you can reach that will help you feel good about yourself as well as give you recognition? If you aren't working currently, can you find a consulting job in which you can use your technical expertise to help a client solve a problem? Write down your ideas.

_____

_____

_____

_____

SELF-KNOWLEDGE

Did you learn something new about yourself during your difficult situation that you were not aware of previously? Did you receive feedback about a specific behavior or skill? Be honest with yourself. Write down what it is along with three ways that you can change or improve it (take a class, identify a mentor, buy a self-help audiotape).

_____

_____

_____

_____

MANAGING RELATIONSHIPS

Did you experience friction or discord with a specific person during your difficult work experience? While some people are truly tough to deal with in the workplace, a relationship involves two people, not just one. What did you learn from your negative experience about the way you handle relationships? If you became involved in a difficult relationship at work again, what would you do differently?

_____

_____

_____

_____

MAINTAINING MOTIVATION

Do you feel focused and energetic about your career? Does the work you've been involved with still interest and stimulate you? If not, write down three to five activities that you can become involved with that would increase your motivation overall. Some suggestions are increasing your exercise routine, taking an art class, researching a new industry, and volunteering for a social cause.

_____

_____

_____

_____

GOAL ORIENTATION

Setting goals is an important part of making changes. Regardless of how severe your Bruised and Gun-shy state is, you must set goals for yourself and your career. Write down two goals that will help you move toward a more optimistic frame of mind. Examples: Completing all the assessments in this book and spending two hours a week researching a new career.

_____

_____

_____

_____

PROFESSIONAL COMMITMENT

Do you feel completely committed to your job and your career? If not, is it because you feel battered by your recent negative work experience or because you no longer have passion for or interest in your career? Write down the things you can do to regain the professional commitment you once had.

_____

_____

_____

_____

CHANGE RESILIENCE

Refer to the results of your self-assessment on handling change on pages 41–42. If you are Bruised and Gun-shy, it is likely your score will reflect this by indicating that you are not comfortable making changes. Identify two positive changes related to work that you can make today or tomorrow which will help you move away from being Bruised and Gun-shy.

_____

_____

_____

_____

INTERESTS

When you think about the work situation that left you feeling Bruised and Gun-shy, how did you feel about the actual work itself? Was the work interesting to you? If so, what about the work interested you/was interesting to you?

_____

_____

_____

_____

Were there aspects of your job that did not interest you? If so, what were they? Describe why they did not interest you.

_____

_____

_____

_____

_____

Step 2: Explore Roadblocks and Opportunities

Once you have determined that you are healing and are more equipped to decide what kind of work situation is right for you, it is time to prepare yourself in case you inadvertently walk into another difficult situation. While this may seem to be a negative approach, the truth is that the likelihood of your being laid off, caught in a merger, or accepting a job with a company whose culture isn't a fit for you is very strong. Even if you decide to start your own business or work as a contractor, there is no guarantee that you will experience success. You are human, after all, and many forces affect your work that you cannot control.

Rupert, a general manager in consumer products, has had a successful career but has had several very difficult patches along the way. While he does admit to being Bruised and Gun-shy, he also says that he has learned how to deal with arduous times in his career that he knows will occur again. In his last position he worked for someone who admitted to Rupert in his first interview that his nickname was the "Yale Terminator." Unfortunately, Rupert ignored this obvious sign that his prospective boss was cruel and took the job anyway because it was a challenging international opportunity. When he left his position, he said that he felt he was in physical danger from his boss. What is Rupert's advice? "Separate what was about you and what was about the other person. Hang on to the fundamental realization that nothing will last forever. Take the position and the work for what it's worth. No matter what you were promised when you were hired, accept it because that's as good as it gets. Manage your expectations." He adds, "You lose a certain elasticity as you move along in your career, and you need to have something to fall back on. Have a support group. For me it's my wife and my kids."

Usually, when people interview for a new job, they look at the job title, location, work responsibilities, and compensation first. Although these factors are important, they are rarely the reason that a job doesn't work out. Instead, the primary reason may be your boss, the company culture, or the job was misrepresented or changed once you were in it. You can help avoid these problems by doing the following before you accept a new job.

1. Assess Your Prospective Boss

Bill DeLeno, a psychotherapist in private practice in White Plains, New York, specializes in helping people with problems at work. He asserts that the number one difficulty people have at work is their boss. One of Bill's patients actually told him he was so afraid of his boss that he couldn't go to his mother's funeral because he had to work.

Not everyone is as obvious as Rupert's new boss, who admitted up front to Rupert what his horrifying nickname was. If you have had a bad experience with a boss, then you will naturally try to learn as much as you can about the person you'll report to in your next job. Even so, few people feel comfortable "interviewing" their possible future boss. Instead, we behave as if the relationship goes one way instead of two. It is important to keep in mind that this person is crucial to your success or failure in your job, so the more you can find out about your prospective new boss before you start working for him or her, the better off you'll be. Remember that bosses usually show their "best face" to you during the interviewing process, especially if they see you as a viable candidate for the job they are trying to fill. If your prospective boss is rude, insensitive, or appears uninterested in you during the interview, this behavior will only become magnified during your working relationship. Asking the following questions will help uncover his or her personality quirks and style:

How would you describe the ideal relationship you could have with someone who reports to you?

What would you expect of me during my first three months at this job? First six months? First year?

How does this align with the organization's expectations? What about its strategy?

What about your job keeps you up at night? How would I help you with the solution to this challenge?

How do you like to communicate and receive information from the people who report to you? How often?

How would you describe your work style?

What should I realistically expect from you as my manager?

Who was the best boss you ever had and why?

What are your top three values?

How do you think people view you within the organization?

Some of these are tough questions to ask; however, an individual's willingness to answer the questions and his or her candor in doing so can be very telling. When you ask any or all of these questions, do so in a nonthreatening way so that your prospective boss isn't turned off.

The most useful information you can get about your prospective boss is from the people who presently work for him or her or have done so in the past. Why is it okay for the people interviewing you to ask you whatever they are legally allowed to and it isn't okay for you? It's not right! Working involves a mutual agreement. Your response to the question "Why do you want to talk with these people?" is the following: "I want a productive relationship that is going to be the best possible fit for both of us. I know what it costs to recruit, hire, and retain an employee, financially and psychologically."

Whoever you question may be cautious about answering, particularly when the answers may not be positive. Again, be sensitive to their position of needing to protect themselves and their job. Read between the lines and probe.

When you are speaking to someone who currently works for or has reported in the past to your prospective boss, ask these questions:

How would you describe your relationship with him?

What are his strengths? What are areas that may need development?

How is he viewed within the organization? Why?

Who is he close to in the organization?

Does he make decisions? Does he involve you in those decisions?

How does he like to communicate (regular meetings, in the hallway, e-mail, reports, voice mail)?

How would you describe his work style?

Does he give feedback? How and when?

What characteristics does he admire?

Does he value and support work/life balance?

How does he deal with conflict?

What are his priorities in his job?

What are his hot buttons or pet peeves?

If he hires me, what advice would you give me to ensure that he and I get started on the right foot?

You will notice that some of these questions are the same as the ones you've asked your prospective boss. Pay attention to which of the answers are the same or similar and which are not.

If your prospective boss is new to the organization, ask him if you can speak to someone at his previous job. Again, if he balks, be concerned.

With the constant change that occurs within organizations, you may not be working for the same person for very long. We all know, however, that even three months of working for someone with whom we don't get along can feel like an eternity!

2. Assess the Company's Culture

Every work environment has its own culture. If you fit into a company's culture—the values employees share, the way people communicate and dress, the behaviors that are accepted—then you probably will have a good working experience. On the other hand, if you don't fit in, regardless of how talented you are at your job or what you've accomplished, the chances are strong that you will either derail voluntarily or be asked to leave the organization.

A company's culture is very powerful and cannot be changed overnight by one person, even a new leader. A culture is an interwoven system of beliefs, values, history, mythology, rituals, and ceremonies. In a work context, these create meaning for people, and although it may not always be easy to describe it to others outside the organization, the company culture definitely influences behavior and the way business is conducted.

Because of this, it is important that you learn how to effectively assess a company's culture to determine if it is a fit for you.

Remember, you spend a lot of time working. There is no reason to be unhappy or to be working in an unsuitable work situation. If you have already had an experience in which you went to work for a company and realized you didn't fit into the culture, you know how painful this can be. Learning how to identify the right culture for you is easy to do if you ask the right questions and rely on your intuition.

Several elements of company culture are important to consider when you are pursuing a new opportunity. One important element is that of values and beliefs. Values and beliefs are principles, standards, or qualities considered inherently worthwhile and desirable. They cannot always be neatly defined in a manual. Values create focus and shape behavior. A historic person in the company (a past leader or pioneer) exemplifies core values and beliefs. Now that you have identified your own top ten values, it will be easier to ask questions in an interview to find out how closely your values match those of your prospective employer.

Think about what you want in a company culture from a "clean slate" perspective, especially if you have never felt as if you fit into a company culture in the past or have had some disappointments. Sit at your computer or take a piece of paper and list the ideal elements that you want and need to feel comfortable in your work environment. Forget about reality for the moment. You can go back to your list later and focus on what you think is realistic.

How do you assess a company's culture? You do it by asking lots of questions; meeting as many people as you can; sitting in the parking lot and observing; sitting in the reception area; looking at the company's Web site, marketing materials, and annual report; and—*most important*—by following your intuition. As a prospective employee you have every right to talk to as many people as you need to, including vendors, clients, and employees who don't work in your functional area. If there is resistance to this, take note and be wary. Remember, if your gut is telling you that something is not quite right, in all likelihood it isn't! It is okay to be excited or interested in a particular job opportunity, but don't fixate on the title, money, perks, or job description and lose sight of the one aspect of the job that can make or break your chances of success: the culture!

At the same time here is a word of caution: "Fit" means the most suitable. You will not find perfection in any job or work situation because it does not exist. Companies are not always completely candid about their cultures. This is another reason to try to talk with as many different people as possible before signing on.

Here are some questions you can ask to assess a company's culture:

How would you describe the culture here?

What is important to senior management here?

How are decisions made? (It could be by senior management only, by consensus, collaboratively, by crisis, or not at all.)

What is the typical background of the people here?

How important is the customer or client?

What kind of hierarchy exists in the company?

What is the preferred method of communication (e-mail, memos, meetings, voice mail, or impromptu hallway conversations)?

Is feedback valued? Does it occur and in what form?

Is innovation or risk-taking valued and rewarded?

How often, when, and why do people leave the company? (Is it of their own volition or are people fired?)

Who are some of the successful people in the company, and why are they successful?

Psychotherapist Bill DeLeno advises that even if you've done a thorough job of assessing a company, "you don't know what you've got until you get there." While it's not easy advice to follow, Bill recommends that if you do find yourself in a situation that is making you very unhappy and you can't seem to change it, "don't linger if it's bad. Every job and work experience is a stepping-stone today anyway."

3. Assess the Job Itself

When you are interviewing for a new job, it is normal to ask questions about the responsibilities you'll have. It is also important to ask questions about the business goals you'll be expected to achieve. Whether you are starting a new job with a company or moving into a new role with your current employer, ask these questions of your boss:

Why does this job exist?

What are your expectations of me in my first three months in this position?

How will you measure my success after a year in this job?

How does this job fit within the department or division?

Who worked in this job before, and where did he or she go?

What did he or she accomplish in this job?

What was difficult for him or her?

What do you think my greatest challenge will be in this job?

What are the three most important business priorities in this job?

Whenever you start a new job or are promoted, create a plan with your new boss and any other stakeholders (which include peers, direct reports, and senior management) who can influence your work and job.

Jackie received a big promotion to run operations for the sales division of her company. Jackie was an assistant controller with no experience in sales. When she was asked what her plans were for her first thirty, sixty, and ninety days, she didn't even have a plan. It hadn't even occurred to her. Not only did she need to understand what her boss was interested in accomplishing, but she was also inheriting a big staff. The first thing she should have done was make an appointment with her new boss and prepare a list of questions for him. She then should have scheduled a one-on-one meeting with every person on her staff to get to know them individually and understand what they had contributed in the past as well as what they would like to do moving forward. Jackie needed to make a strong first impression on everyone in her new role because the department was experiencing problems and because initially Jackie wouldn't have seemed an obvious choice for the job.

Once Jackie gathered all this information and started to develop relationships, she needed to set goals that were measurable and realistic, and have her boss and other stakeholders sign off on them. Going forward, Jackie should meet with everyone at least every forty-five to sixty days. If possible, she should make an ally out of the person who was previously in her role.

It is just as important to continue assessing your job once you've been doing it for a while. While most people who are laid off from their jobs aren't fired because of performance, people do lose their jobs because business priorities shift. With this shift comes the assumption that different skills may be needed. Most companies aren't very good at assessing their employees' skills and putting them in a different role that will benefit both employees and their company. Often a person is hired to accomplish one thing, and if the needs of the organization change, that person may no longer be viewed as relevant to the company's new priorities. Sometimes it is difficult to know whether you are still viewed as integral to the company's priorities. How can you be aware of this in your company so that you are not caught off guard? Unfortunately, very few people are aware that they may be losing their job before they actually do. Sadly, very few people take care of the things that they can control before they lose their job. As a result, the recovery period takes much longer.

What can you do to stay aware of the status of your job? In *Are You a Corporate Refugee?* Ruth Luban talks about the "signposts" that signify the first phase of being a corporate refugee—what she calls "On the Brink"—when you know something is amiss at your company. Some of the signposts that Luban describes are such things as frequent reorganizations; budget cuts; vacancies left unfulfilled; not being invited to planning meetings you used to attend; a boss who doesn't have time to meet with you; and a merger or buyout of your company.

Instead of burying your head in the sand in an effort to avoid what might be happening, Luban recommends some ways that you can replace your feelings of uncertainty with structure. She suggests that engaging in these practical activities will equip you for the possibility that the signposts are indeed leading to the loss of your job. Here are some of her recommendations:

Start networking with recruiters, your competition, former colleagues, and trade associations.

Get organized by cleaning out your desk files and computer files, and updating your Rolodex.

Use your benefits by scheduling all those doctors' appointments you've been putting off. Staying healthy is even more important when you're going through this stressful time.

Simplify your life by reducing clutter and winnowing down scheduled activities.

Reorganize your finances by assessing your savings and looking at areas where you can cut expenses, and avoid using credit cards.

Taking action in these areas will help you feel more in control and less stressed in the event that you do lose your job.

Step 3: Create an Action Plan

Now that you've looked at what you learned from your past work experiences and determined what you want from your next job, it is important to create a plan to move ahead.

Answer the following questions:

What do you want your work to look like in three months? Six months? A year? Describe it as specifically as you can.

Three months

_____

_____

_____

Six months

_____

_____

_____

A year

_____

_____

_____

What steps do you need to take to make this happen? What kind of research should you do? What resources do you need to move forward?

Steps to take (update your résumé, set up meetings with your network, have a conversation with your current boss):

_____

_____

_____

_____

Research to do (learn about a new industry, interview several people who are working in a job that you'd like to do):

_____

_____

_____

_____

Resources you need (buy a new computer, find a mentor):

_____

_____

_____

_____

Do you want to be on your own? If this is the route you think you'd like to take, it is even more important to recover from feeling Bruised and Gun-shy because planning and starting a new business will tap all your energy and many of your resources.

———————

Pat was a managing counsel for a major commercial bank. She had a great job but had been doing it for twenty years. She stayed because she liked the work and it was near her home and two children. But then the bank began to sell off assets in her area. Pat was downsized two weeks before she turned fifty. "I was traumatized at first and started looking for a job with another large financial company, although everyone told me that I should be in my own business. I took some private clients during my job search. I loved it and decided to go into business for myself. That's a very risky thing to do at my age, since I need to maintain a certain income level and my husband is not making a lot. But it has turned out to be a very rewarding second career."

Ask yourself the following questions:

If you want to be on your own, what kind of work do you want to do?

_____

_____

_____

_____

How will you begin the process of planning your own business? (Read chapter 9, "Yearning to Be on Your Own," first!)

_____

_____

_____

_____

How will you manage stress and maintain your psychological well-being (take yoga classes, write in your journal, spend extra time with your family)?

_____

_____

_____

_____

Before she was fired, Susie worked in sales. Her employer and another larger company merged, and she was let go for "political" reasons. "I stayed a year longer than I should have," Susie admits, "because I was determined to make it work." Her counsel to others? "Remember who you are. Remember what successes you've had in the past. Don't let anyone strip away your self-confidence. Stay whole."

List three successes you've had in your career that you are especially proud of:

_____

_____

_____

_____

Whatever your current and future work choices are for yourself—staying in your present job, changing careers, starting a business, or retiring—think of what you've learned from the difficult working situations you have experienced. Use these lessons to be more prepared to deal with losing your job, working for a difficult boss, or experiencing a merger. While much of what has happened to you in the past may have been out of your control, if you are clear about what you need and can tolerate in your next work situation, you will feel more in control should you get involved in another difficult situation.

CHAPTER 8

Bored and Plateaued

Most of us have felt bored or unchallenged at some point in our lives, whether for a few hours, several months, or even years at a time. If you have been involved in the same kind of work for a while, you've probably reached the top of your game from a competency standpoint. It feels good to be viewed by your professional peers, friends, and family as an expert in your field. Chances are you also enjoy many perks, including healthy compensation, status, and the overall feeling of having "made it" in your career.

But the picture might not be completely rosy. You may be so comfortable that you have begun to feel plateaued, which is to say stifled, unchallenged, or bored. Not only do you feel listless, restless, aimless, or disengaged with the tasks you are performing or the people you work with, but you also exhibit "bored" behaviors. These behaviors may include making a lot of personal calls and e-mailing your friends, chatting online, taking at least a half-dozen coffee and food breaks, and fantasizing about becoming the next million-dollar lottery winner and telling your boss that you're quitting your job. When you're bored and your coworkers don't seem to be bored, you naturally feel alienated and weird.

Feeling bored or plateaued can occur gradually so that you are able to shrug it off for a time, or it may come on suddenly and linger chronically so that it isn't quite as easy to ignore. If you are feeling bored, you may not necessarily be feeling plateaued. If you are experiencing one of these feelings, however, you are probably susceptible to the other as well.

Being bored or plateaued does not mean that you aren't working hard or that you don't have enough work to do. Being busy and dealing with the excessive stimulation that the workplace provides us with today have little to do with being bored. The combination of the two merely leads to a greater level of burnout.

Through more than ten years of conducting career development workshops, author and consultant Kurt Sandholtz has gathered extensive data on why and how people become Bored and Plateaued. He explains that most people typically pass through three phases during the course of their careers: (1) low skill and high passion; (2) high passion and high skill; and (3) high skill and low passion. Sandholtz's phase 3 is a great shorthand description for Bored and Plateaued. Although being Bored and Plateaued is more likely to happen to someone who is more senior in his or her career, it can happen at any age.

Psychologist Judith Bardwick, author of *The Plateauing Trap: How to Avoid It in Your Career and in Your Life*, uses the phrase "structural plateauing" to describe the end of promotions and "content plateauing" to depict the end of growth and learning. Similarly, Kurt Sandholtz labels these two types of plateauing as position plateauing and contribution plateauing. Regardless of what terms we use to describe it, the reality is that corporations today are unable to offer the kinds of promotional opportunities they could fifteen or twenty years ago. This is a reflection of both corporate downsizing and a gradual elimination of the promotional ladder. Many of us already have and will continue to experience this corporate "ceiling," while all of us can face, as Sandholtz points out, the end of promotions, which naturally occurs eventually in a career.

When you were promoted in the past, you knew that with that promotion would come new experiences, different relationships, and the opportunity to develop new skills. If you have been in the same job for several years or haven't learned anything new for a while, it is easy to become stifled by repetition and disinterested in the overfamiliar tasks you routinely perform. Although it is normal for a productive person to experience such feelings on occasion, there are many negative ramifications of being in this predicament, particularly long-term. For one thing, it becomes increasingly difficult to hide your feelings from your boss, peers, subordinates, and clients. Rachelle, a senior human resources director, recalls being pulled aside by her boss and asked if she wanted to take some extended time off because she didn't seem engaged in her work the way she used to be. She expressed surprise that her boss had picked up on her boredom so easily.

If you have been in the same job for a while, without the benefit of ongoing continuing education opportunities, your skills may become outdated and you could be viewed by others as someone who is no longer "state-of-the-art." Research has shown over and over again, that the healthiest, most productive adult is the one who is constantly learning and growing, not the one who is stagnant.

Working in a job or career where you are Bored and Plateaued can produce many negative emotional, psychological, and physical effects. Feeling depressed, anxious, unmotivated, or frustrated not only impacts your work but also the rest of your life, including your significant relationships and even your health.

Barbara, a forty-year-old senior financial analyst, has been in the same role for three years and is so bored with her job that she thinks of reasons not to go to work. Her boredom at work has also eroded the quality of her personal life. Barbara, who is single, isn't interested in going on vacation and feels so boring that she can't imagine why anyone would date her. She has gradually gained weight during the last several years and isn't doing anything to lose it. Barbara is so plateaued in her life that she is simply waiting for someone or something to motivate her to make the changes she knows she needs to make.

If you like your field or aspects of the work you do but have mastered the essentials and are hungry to learn new things, you are probably Bored and Plateaued. It is time to learn what you can do to change your feelings from Bored and Plateaued to committed, creative, competent, and energized. Remember also that many people feel bored or stifled at some point in their career, so it's important to analyze your situation carefully and identify the culprit—what is really boring you—before taking action to eliminate those feelings.

Step 1: Complete the "Bored and Plateaued" Self-Assessment

Flip back to the self-assessments you took on interests on pages 51–55 and favorite skills on pages 56–60. Review your responses.

Now it's time to look at your current work situation. Answer the questions below. Your goal is to identify your interests and favorite skills that are being satisfied in your job currently and to think of ways to eliminate some of the things that are causing you to feel Bored and Plateaued.

1. How would you describe what you do for a living? Avoid using a title of any kind.

   _____

   _____

   _____

   _____

2. Which of your favorite skills do you use most frequently in your current position? (Refer to your list of favorite skills in chapter 4.)

   _____

   _____

_____

_____

3. What do you like the most about your job (tangible or intangible)?

_____

_____

_____

_____

4. How could you augment this aspect of your job? Be specific.

_____

_____

_____

_____

5. What do you like least about your job (tangible or intangible)?

_____

_____

_____

_____

6. Can you find a way to reduce or eliminate this aspect? If so, describe how.

_____

_____

_____

_____

7. Describe your feelings of boredom.

_____

_____

_____

_____

8. Describe why you feel plateaued.

_____

_____

_____

_____

9. Do you currently have any specific career goals? If so, what are they?

_____

_____

_____

_____

10. What do you believe are the obstacles preventing you from moving out of your Bored and Plateaued situation?

_____

_____

_____

_____

11. What could help you move into a fulfilling and rewarding work situation?

_____

_____

_____

_____

Answering these basic questions should help you understand your current work situation more clearly. You will refer to your answers later.

Step 2: Explore Roadblocks and Opportunities

Wanda was a forty-year-old vice president of marketing in the consumer products industry who was "bored silly" and felt stuck in her job. She was unchallenged and not using her strengths, and because she had been in this Bored and Plateaued phase for several years, she was not motivated to make a career change although she desperately wanted to. Wanda dreamed of being an interior designer or working in the fashion industry.

When Wanda finally began to do something about her feelings, she took a series of assessments. They revealed that she is extroverted, intuitive, makes decisions based on her values, and prefers spontaneity. Her primary values are creativity and autonomy. A typical baby boomer, she is concerned about earning less money than she does now, and because she hasn't saved much, she isn't willing to decrease her compensation dramatically. She is single, and although she works hard when challenged, she is very interested in attaining a balanced lifestyle. Since she estimates that she will have to work for another twenty-five years, Wanda wants to move into a field that offers a variety of opportunities for her to work flexibly and long-term.

When Wanda answered the questions listed on pages 128–31, she discovered the chances were slim that she would ever muster the interest or energy to change something about her current job to alleviate her boredom. The truth is that although she knew her business well and was very comfortable, she just couldn't bring herself to think of ways to revitalize her situation to make it work for her. She yearned to leave consumer products marketing. Fortunately, she knew that she was interested in the interior design and fashion fields. She was also pretty clear about what her skills were—in the areas of marketing, operations, and working with clients. Because she was certain that just changing her current situation wouldn't alleviate her boredom and that she wanted to move out of her field altogether, she was faced with the prospect of changing careers. Wanda's first obstacle was believing that it was actually possible for her to switch fields without taking a significant cut in pay. She was especially worried about having to accept an entry-level position with an entry-level salary. Initially, this fear slowed her down. Like many prospective career changers, Wanda put obstacles in her own way to mask her fear of the unknown. In his book *The Pathfinder*, Nicholas Lore calls these manufactured obstacles "Yeahbuts." He lists twenty-five or so, including "I don't have enough talent," "I'm too young/too stupid," "I'm not committed enough," "I'm over-/under-educated," "I'm over-/under-qualified," and "I have too much/too little experience."

Yet once Wanda had made up her mind that changing fields was what she was going to do, her entire attitude shifted and she felt excited about her next career. She began brainstorming ways to meet people in the interior design and fashion industries so that she could learn more about the kinds of opportunities that might exist for her. Wanda started networking with people in her two target industries. She didn't spend a lot of time doing it, but every week she would talk on the phone or meet with someone in interior design or fashion. As she became immersed in this process, her excitement grew, confirming that she was correct in her original assessment: She should be working in fashion or interior design. Interestingly, once Wanda found the motivation to change careers, she wasn't nearly as focused on the issue of compensation.

Every once in a while Wanda's energy flagged, and she would stop networking. When this happened, she would identify one simple action step to reignite the spark, which would help her feel motivated once again. Then, after three months, Wanda ran into Ursula, a friend from high school, and as she did with everyone, she told her what she was trying to do. Her friend reminded Wanda that another mutual friend, Cynthia, whom Wanda hadn't seen in a long time, owned an agency for designers in New York City. Wanda met with Cynthia, who gave her several names of people to contact in the design industry. Wanda started calling them. Not long afterward she heard from Cynthia, who asked if she would be interested in running sales for her business, since the person in that position was going on maternity leave and not planning to return. Wanda jumped at the opportunity and has been happily working for Cynthia for nearly two years. She feels incredibly fulfilled, and—the icing on the cake—is making exactly the same salary she was earning in her former career!

Wanda is an example of someone who changed her Bored and Plateaued status by leaving her job and her industry. The first thing you should do if you are feeling Bored and Plateaued is take a look at your current situation.

Favorite Skills

How did you respond to the question "What favorite skills do you use most frequently?" Whatever favorite skills you identified, would you feel more engaged and interested if you could increase the time you spent using these? If you like to write but write only business memos and e-mail messages, is there a way to increase the amount of writing you do by starting a division newsletter or approaching your local newspaper to write a monthly column?

Take a look at the favorite skills you wrote down on pages 58–59 and think of different opportunities you could create to make them a bigger part of your work life. Write down every possible opportunity you come up with. For the moment forget about any obstacles you perceive that could prevent you from making it happen.

_____

_____

_____

_____

_____

_____

_____

Tasks

Take a look at your list of things you least enjoy in your work from page 129. Doing tasks that we don't enjoy can lead to boredom and ultimately to unhappiness. Put on your creative hat and think of ways to get these tasks off your plate. Is there someone to whom you could delegate them—an intern, assistant, junior staff member, outside vendor, or peer—who enjoys that type of work more than you do? If you could eliminate or reduce these tasks you don't enjoy, and spend your time doing other things, would you be less bored? Write down the list of tasks along with ideas for delegating or eliminating them.

_____

_____

_____

_____

_____

Remember When You Weren't Bored?

Can you think back and recall when you began to feel bored in your work? Did boredom creep up on you slowly, or was it triggered by a specific incident or situation? Write down how you think it would feel if you were no longer bored in your work. If you can't imagine what that would feel like, look back on your career and try to recall a time when you felt energized and challenged. How was your situation then different from the situation you're in now?

_____

_____

_____

_____

_____

_____

Revitalizing Your Current Situation

Despite being Bored and Plateaued, you may decide to stay with your current employer for a year or two more, or you may not. If you're leaning toward leaving your present job, before you do, make sure you have explored what you could change in your current job situation that could alleviate your current state.

How? First, be clear about what you'd like to change before you approach other people in your organization. Also be sure that you are able to communicate what the benefit is to your employer. Let's take Rachelle's situation, mentioned earlier. Rachelle's boss had asked her if she wanted to take time off because she seemed bored and disinterested in her work. Rachelle grabbed the opportunity. After taking three weeks off and traveling, Rachelle realized that she really loved human resources and just needed a new challenge. Although she did begin to conduct a job search outside her company, Rachelle, who loves to travel, ended up interviewing for and accepting a human resources director position for her current employer, in which she provides support for the company's Latin American division. In her new job she works in a function she loves and has more autonomy. She feels energized and stimulated, quite different from the way she felt just six months before she started her new position.

Rachelle is fortunate that she works for a company large enough to provide internal job opportunities for its employees. Her employer realized that Rachelle, a talented HR professional with exceptional people skills and an understanding of the complex political workings of the organization, was an asset to the company and an employee worth keeping.

Even though you may work for a smaller company, if you and your employer are creative, you will find ways to add new and different responsibilities to your current job and prepare an exciting new job description. Most Bored and Plateaued people immediately think about leaving their company rather than finding a way to change their present work situation. But leaving isn't always the answer. If your employer values you, then it is in his or her best interest to keep you and to help you find a way to reenergize yourself, for the benefit of the organization. If not, there is a company out there that *will* appreciate you.

Changing the dynamics of your job may or may not be the solution to your Bored and Plateaued state. Learning something new can be an effective hedge against boredom, but those familiar feelings may return once you've mastered a new skill or successfully taken on a new challenge. That is why it's so critical to analyze the source of your Bored and Plateaued feelings before applying what could turn out to be merely a Band-Aid solution.

Staying in Your Industry

If you have investigated changing your work or moving into a new position at your current company but there are real obstacles to making this happen or you really don't want to change careers right now, there are several other options you can explore. The most obvious is to find a new position in your current industry— either the same type of job you have now or a different role in another company. Be cautious about using this tactic. Consider the case of Donna. She was a human resource generalist for a publishing company. After six years she was bored but decided to "hang in" because of rumors of an impending takeover of her company by another publishing house. Sure enough, this occurred, and Donna received a nice severance package. After taking the summer off, she started her job search. Results from assessments and feedback from several friends helped Donna discover that she had the ideal personality for sales. Although sales sounded appealing to her, the thought of leaving HR and taking a risk made her nervous, so she accepted the first offer she received—as an HR generalist at a relocation company. Unfortunately, it was a bad fit. Donna couldn't relate to the employees and was uncomfortable not only with the way they communicated but with many other aspects of the company culture. She decided to quit, without having another job, and then worked as a temporary recruiter for six months. Again she conducted a job search and, ignoring the voice in her head and her friends' advice, accepted yet another HR generalist position in the publishing industry. Although this time the firm's culture is comfortable for Donna, she is back where she was almost two years ago. Sitting at her desk, she is still thinking about how to find the courage to leave human resources and go into sales. Unfortunately, Donna is plagued with doubts and keeps hearing the message she received growing up: Find a good job with a decent salary and stick with it through thick and thin.

David is another example of someone who is Bored and Plateaued. Having been in the entertainment industry for ten years, he was bored. At the beginning of each new job (he has had three), he wasn't at all bored because he had to adjust to a different culture, get to know new players, and learn new skills. When he really explored the root of his boredom, however, David discovered that throughout his career he had been using many skills that he really wasn't interested in using, and he wasn't using others that he loved. David determined that he wanted to write more, develop creative messages or promotional campaigns, and function in a more persuasive role. He also had a deep interest in current affairs, politics, and media. David created a list of favorite skills that he wanted to be using every day; he identified public affairs, public relations, and media consulting as avenues to explore. Once he identified these new areas, he felt excited and very committed.

Changing jobs in your industry makes sense if you love the industry and haven't yet accomplished the things you'd like to accomplish or learned everything you could. It also makes sense if you're unable to move into a role that interests you within your current company. If this is what you want, be very focused and adamant about communicating to prospective employers in your industry that you will move only if you are given a role that is different from the one you currently have. Otherwise, it is likely that you'll be bored after six months to a year and be back to where you were before you changed jobs.

Focusing on the World Outside of Work

Another solution to overcoming boredom or lack of learning in your work is to focus your energy on the world outside of your job. As adults we all have interests or untapped talents that we've allowed to fade because of our work and family responsibilities. Take a look at the results of your interests self-assessment and select one thing that jumps out at you. Plan to take a class, hire a coach, or attend a workshop. It is not recommended that you ignore your Bored and Plateaued state at work indefinitely, but revitalizing yourself in another area of your life can energize your personal life now and your career later on.

By getting involved in something that you find fun, exciting, interesting, or fulfilling, you may discover the key to ending boredom in your career. You also may learn how to weave your outside interests into your work. This can be accomplished in several ways.

One option is to immerse yourself in your interest outside of work while working your "day job" to satisfy your need to earn a living. Robert is an example. An avid foxhunter who owns two horses, he spends nearly all his spare time either foxhunting or socializing with other foxhunters. During the week, however, he puts on business clothes and drives into Atlanta to his job as a contingency recruiter for an agency. While he doesn't particularly like his job, he earns a good living, which allows him to support his expensive outside interest. This is an easy trade-off for him to make since his enjoyment of foxhunting far outweighs the boredom he feels at his job.

Another option is to do as Julia did: eventually find a way to turn your passion into a full-time job. For eight years Julia did speaking engagements on such topics as sales, networking, and career management for local associations for free, simply because she enjoyed giving talks. Every year the number of speeches she gave increased. Several years ago, when she was at a crossroad in her sales career, she was having lunch with an acquaintance who commented that Julia lit up when she talked about public speaking. That moment changed Julia's life. Soon after that lunch, she began to make plans to speak professionally. It had never occurred to her that public speaking was what she should do for a living. Until that moment Julia simply thought of it as a fun hobby.

Turning an avocation into a vocation can be a scary proposition; doing it successfully requires planning that includes preparing yourself psychologically and financially. After that fateful lunch, Julia spent eight months working in a transitional job she disliked while planning and priming herself to start her professional speaking practice. As stressful as Julia's "for the time being" job was, the income and structure it offered made her transition much smoother and less frightening.

If you can't shake the feeling that "it just isn't fun anymore," as Kurt Sandholtz says, because you're stuck in phase 3—high skill, low passion—now is the time to realize it, accept it, and start moving forward. Start small by learning something new, or, as Sandholtz suggests, start looking at your job from the outside in and think about how you can approach it differently. And if that doesn't nip your boredom in the bud, start the exhilarating process of changing your career.

Step 3: Create an Action Plan

As you figure out how you intend to eliminate your Bored and Plateaued situation, you need to have clear answers to the following questions.

What are the reasons for your boredom with work?

_____

_____

_____

_____

How can you revitalize or change your current job or working situation so that you won't be bored?

_____

_____

_____

_____

Do you want to pursue a different job within your industry? If so, how will you do this?

_____

_____

_____

_____

What are the reasons that you would accept another job in your industry?

_____

_____

_____

_____

Have you decided to change careers and leave your industry? If so, write down what steps you will take in the following four areas:

Self-assessment

_____

_____

_____

_____

Research

_____

_____

_____

_____

Writing your résumé

_____

_____

_____

_____

Writing or updating your social networking media profiles

_____

_____

_____

_____

Networking to learn about the industry you're interested in and to uncover job openings

_____

_____

_____

_____

Do you have a hobby or interest that you'd like to spend more time with? If so, what do you need to do to make this happen?

_____

_____

_____

_____

Regardless of what you decide to do first, it is important that you do something—anything—to begin to alleviate your feeling of boredom. Use your Bored and Plateaued state as a launchpad to new and satisfying work. The choice is yours.

CHAPTER 9

Yearning to Be on Your Own

If you are dreaming of starting your own business, you are not alone. A survey conducted by the accounting firm Ernst & Young found that 78 percent of influential Americans believe that entrepreneurship will be the defining trend of the twenty-first century. Why is this so? The study identified six factors as the primary reasons that a growing number of people are thinking about, planning, and starting their own businesses:

1. Technology
2. Economic conditions
3. Social conditions
4. A global economy
5. Government deregulation
6. Inability of large corporations to innovate

In a 2009 survey by FindLaw.com, 61 percent of Americans said that they have either started or thought about starting a small business. According to an interview by *Success* magazine, Stephanie Rahlfs of FindLaw.com concludes, "Even in difficult economic times, people often take advantage of opportunities to start a business where they see unmet needs—or the chance to turn a passion or interest into a business—or because they want to have more control and responsibility over their work life."

Then there are the thousands of Americans who have become what the *New York Times* has coined accidental entrepreneurs. These are people who find themselves out of work with no viable option except to make it on their own through self-employment.

The number of people thinking about or already working in their own business is also increasing across demographic groups. According to *The Futurist* magazine, baby boomers, considered to be the healthiest and most educated generation in history, started retiring from their traditional careers or were laid off in the recession of 2008, and a large number have or will start their own businesses.

Both Gen Xers and Millennials are naturally more entrepreneurial in spirit, and they don't hesitate to start their own businesses. Neither Gen Xers nor Millennials view starting a business as a risky venture the way many baby boomers might.

In 2007 there were 27.2 million privately owned businesses in the United States. In 2008 small businesses in the United States represented 99.7 percent of all employer firms. If you are thinking about starting your own business, what is motivating you to do so? You have heard the cliché "You can be your own boss" touted as the overriding benefit of "running your own show." It is true that you have no one to hold accountable but yourself for what you either achieve or fail to achieve in your own business.

Consider these other reasons:

Catherine, an independent contractor who handles marketing for a catalog company, says, "I like the freedom that comes from working for myself."

Leonard, an author, journalist, and psychotherapist who earned his master's degree in counseling at age fifty-two, says, "I am on my own and am quite aware of the drawbacks, such as a lack of resources and a lonely feeling at times. But I get more of a sense of meaning from my work by being on my own."

Barri worked as chief operating officer of a $12 million start-up company and became ill. She left, took a four-year sabbatical, and then tried to go back to work at a Fortune 500 company. "I knew it was a mistake almost the day I started." Now, says Barri, "I'm back on my own doing business consulting and enjoying it."

Maria runs her own training and consulting business. "Having my own practice allows me the freedom to 'mix and match' my skills and experience. I also have the privilege of organizing my own time and tasks. I work with Japanese companies and often answer e-mails well into the night—but then I have the time in the morning to go to water aerobics and privately teach English as a second language (ESL) students!"

In an article in *Success* magazine, Lori Rosenkopf, assistant professor of management at the Wharton School, says, "You don't have to have misplaced priorities, a dysfunctional personality, and a fanatical work ethic to be a thriving entrepreneur. The creation of value through innovative products and services—the essence of entrepreneurship—can happen for any sort of person. You can be a successful entrepreneur no matter who you are."

Being self-employed can take many different forms, from buying a company or franchise to working as a contract employee or starting a consulting business. Regardless of which of these self-employment options you choose, it is crucial to your success to become very familiar with your preferences, skills, interests, and the areas that you need to develop.

Step 1: Complete the "Yearning to Be on Your Own" Self-Assessment

It is important for you to be clear about your reasons for wanting to be on your own. By revisiting your self-assessment results, you can confirm your strengths, weaknesses, needs, and desires in relation to being on your own.

Review the values you wrote down on page 33 . Which ones do

you think you can fulfill by being self-employed? Which of these values might not be as easily fulfilled by being on your own?

CHANGE RESILIENCE

How did you score on the change resilience quiz on pages 41–42? As an entrepreneur you will be dealing constantly with change in your business—with your customers and clients, with competitors in the marketplace, and with the economy.

If your score indicated that you have a high level of discomfort with change, think about some ways that you can become more comfortable with change. One suggestion is to start making small changes in your routine starting today. How can you begin to be more comfortable with change?

_____

_____

_____

_____

INTERESTS

Turning an interest into a business is very common. Review the ten interests you listed in the self-assessment you took on page 51. How can you incorporate one or several of these into your own business?

FAVORITE SKILLS

One reason you may want to be on your own is that you have tired of doing work or undertaking projects which aren't interesting to you anymore. While many entrepreneurs will tell you that as a small business owner you will become the "chief cook and bottle washer," you gain a higher level of satisfaction even by doing tedious tasks, because it is your business. Nevertheless, it is important to understand which of your favorite skills you prefer using so that you can plan your entrepreneurial situation more effectively. Review the top ten favorite skills you listed in the self-assessment on pages 58–59. Which of these do you want to spend the majority of your time being involved with? Write them down below:

_____

_____

_____

_____

_____

Having a strong desire to be in your own business is very important. In addition, studies of successful entrepreneurs reveal common characteristics: motivations, attitudes, personality traits, values, and beliefs. How well suited are you to being an entrepreneur? Take this brief quiz to begin to find out.

HOW DO YOU KNOW SELF-EMPLOYMENT IS FOR YOU?

1. Security isn't a very high need of mine.

Agree   *Disagree*

2. I become easily bored with many things I undertake.

Agree   *Disagree*

3. I am willing to commit my savings to starting my own business.

Agree   *Disagree*

4. I am willing to borrow money from others if need be.

Agree   *Disagree*

5. I am very tired of a daily routine and really would like more variety.

Agree   *Disagree*

6. I am willing to work as long and as hard as it takes to launch my business.

Agree   *Disagree*

7. The idea of selling doesn't scare me.

Agree   *Disagree*

8. I truly see the value of networking and am willing to do it constantly.

Agree   *Disagree*

9. As a child or younger person I started one or several entrepreneurial ventures.

Agree   *Disagree*

10. I enjoy spending time alone.

Agree   *Disagree*

11. I prefer solo or one-on-one activities to group activities.

Agree   *Disagree*

12. My work history shows a consistent pattern of stretching myself by plunging into new situations and learning new skills.

Agree   *Disagree*

13. Although realistic, I'm an optimistic person.

Agree   *Disagree*

14. My spouse or significant other and family are supportive of me.

Agree   *Disagree*

15. I am a decisive person who is willing to make quick decisions even when I don't have all the information.

Agree   *Disagree*

16. I'm usually pretty good about asking other people for help or mentoring when I'm unsure or lack knowledge about something.

Agree   *Disagree*

17. Others describe me as a focused person.

Agree   *Disagree*

18. I am able to motivate myself consistently and maintain a high level of motivation even when under stress.

Agree   *Disagree*

19. I have the emotional ability to bounce back pretty quickly after setbacks or failure.

Agree   *Disagree*

20. When I face problems or challenges, I feel inspired to solve them.

Agree   *Disagree*

SCORE

Now add up the number of Agrees you circled.

15 to 20:   You have the mind-set of an entrepreneur and should be able to achieve wonderful success in your own venture. Although your entrepreneurial instincts are good, be sure to write a solid business plan.

10 to 14:   If you are very thorough about writing a business plan, securing financing, and getting support from your family and network, you have a very good chance for success in your own business.

9 to 13:   While you need to learn more about being self-employed, with focused passion and some education you can be successful. Perhaps you should find a partner or work as a contract employee for additional support first.

5 to 8:   Your skills and attitudes are not indicative of entrepreneurial success. If you are yearning to be on your own, you should seriously consider taking some classes, finding a mentor who is self-employed, and examining your attitudes before taking the plunge.

1 to 4:   Your score indicates that your talents may not lie in the entrepreneurial arena. Take another look at what you feel is missing in your work and think of a different approach—besides starting a business—to fulfill your needs.

Regardless of whether your score is 20 or 1, if you undertake a business on your own, you will experience many challenges and obstacles along with the joy and rewards. Making a career shift to entrepreneurism is riskier than staying in the corporate world, so be sure to question your own motives carefully.

While many people think that having their own business automatically enables them to earn more money than they ever have before, this may not turn out to be true. While the need to feed and clothe yourself and your family may be very real, a truly successful entrepreneur always has a higher purpose than earning money. You may have decided that starting your own business, rather than working as an employee for someone else, is the only way to fulfill your need for meaning. In fact, 90 percent of the people interviewed for this book who yearned to be self-employed ranked the need to find meaning as having more importance than the desire to earn a lot of money. These individuals realized that they could find their version of meaning more easily through their own business than through someone else's.

Step 2: Exploring Roadblocks and Opportunities

So you've made the decision to strike out on your own. What next? The good news is that there are a number of options to pursue under the umbrella of entrepreneurial ventures:

· You can opt to work as a temporary or interim employee, either in a long-term contract with one company or a series of short stints for many different organizations.

· You can "hang out your shingle" as a sole practitioner and sell a product or provide a service. The term "soloist" became popular in the late 1990s to describe a businessperson who is more involved with doing the actual work than in building, growing, and eventually selling a business. Consultants also belong to this group. George Gendron, former editor in chief of *Inc.* magazine, calls this type of individual "a knowledge worker."

· You may decide to join the thousands of entrepreneurs who have purchased franchises. While the concept of a franchise can be appealing because of the brand that is already in place for you and the promise of training and support, there are other factors to consider, such as the up-front investment of capital, the lack of complete control over how you run your business, stiff competition, and the lifestyle of a franchise owner. These are areas you will need to research and think about carefully.

· Buying an established business that is healthy or one that needs turning around is yet another route to take. There are plenty of businesses for sale. Buying a business is sometimes referred to as "secondhand" entrepreneurship because the start-up phase is eliminated.

· Finding one or more partners and creating a limited partnership or incorporating your business is another choice. If either of these options appeals to you, you are probably serious about building a company.

How do you decide which option is right for you? Below are some pros and cons of each of the five types of entrepreneurial ventures described above, some assessments to help you determine which route is best for you, as well as some steps you will need to take toward achieving each venture.

Working as a Contract Employee

As a contract or contingent employee, your focus is on identifying a company that needs your specific set of skills, which enables you to negotiate your compensation as well as how and when you will deliver the work. Your mutual goal is to produce immediate results for the company. The pluses? If you want a flexible schedule, need to beef up your résumé, or are interested in trying out a certain type of work before pursuing it as a full-time employee, then becoming a contractor could be the right career move for you.

Ann is a human resources professional. At sixty-two she has found it increasingly difficult to find full-time employment. During the boom economy of the late twentieth and early twenty-first centuries, Ann held a series of contract recruiting positions with various Fortune 500 companies and is thrilled that she can include these blue-chip companies on her résumé. Ann possesses a very marketable skill and as a result she has had very little "bench time."

Yet, as Ann learned, this type of work has its downside. As a contract worker you don't usually have benefits such as health insurance and paid vacation time, nor do you have the affiliation and status you had as a full-time employee. Any company that hires you as a contractor will expect you to possess state-of-the-art skills in your field, skills that you must acquire on your own time from training that you pay for out of your own pocket. Once your current assignment has ended, you face the challenge of marketing yourself to new prospective employers. Since Ann has had health insurance benefits with only one of the companies she has worked for as a contract recruiter, she worries about not having ongoing health coverage at her age. And she is particularly vulnerable to the swings in the economy. During the most recent recession when employee layoffs at large corporations occurred, Ann found it more and more difficult to find contract recruiting positions.

Wally is an accountant who, feeling Bored and Plateaued, finally decided to leave his employer of several years when the company was taken over by new management. Wally made sure that his separation arrangement with his employer included a severance package. Because he was unsure of what he wanted to do next, Wally decided to temp and immediately found an accounting assignment. No sooner did he start his new assignment than he realized the work bored him. Wally fulfilled his time commitment and then began another six-month assignment for a start-up company. This time he is enjoying himself and feels challenged for the first time in years. In fact, Wally is having so much fun that he hasn't decided whether or not he'll continue working as an independent contractor. Even if he decides to go to work for a company full-time after this assignment ends, Wally will approach the job market with a renewed sense of enthusiasm for his work.

Working as a Sole Practitioner

If you decide to start a business on your own without the structure of a franchise or the support of a partner, you have the advantage of being able to change gears whenever necessary to meet marketplace needs. On the other hand, you'll need to present the professional image of a company despite the fact that you *are* the company.

When you become a sole practitioner, your greatest challenge initially is to decide on, and commit to, what it is you will provide to customers or clients, whether it be a product, a service, or both. While it may be very clear to you that, for example, as a CPA you will provide accounting services, you still need to ask yourself a number of questions. Do you want to specialize in serving individuals or small businesses? If you want to focus on small businesses, do you want to help small businesses in service industries only? What kinds of service industries? Where will you concentrate geographically? Is there a specific type of accounting work that you won't do because you dislike it? Conversely, do you love working in a specific niche of accounting and think you would like to specialize in it?

Answering the following questions carefully will help you narrow your business focus.

1. Do you have specific technical skills and motivated abilities that you would enjoy using in your own business? What are they? Who needs these?

   _____

   _____

   _____

   _____

2. Is there a glaring need in the marketplace that is either unfilled or burgeoning? If so, what is it?

   _____

   _____

   _____

   _____

3. Does a current trend exist in the marketplace that has created a need for, or different approach to, an established product or service? What about an anticipated trend? If so, what is it?

   _____

   _____

_____

_____

4. Is there a very specific niche that you can fill either because of your unique skills or a market need? What is it?

_____

_____

_____

_____

5. Is there an existing product or service that you know could be improved? Describe it.

_____

_____

_____

_____

6. Is there an established service or product that can be introduced in a different market? What is it?

_____

_____

_____

_____

7. Have you observed recurring buying patterns of individuals or corporations that can create a business opportunity for you? What are they?

_____

_____

_____

_____

8. Is there a business in another country that you could expand globally?

_____

_____

_____

_____

Answering these questions requires some serious thought and market research. It is impossible to really know what the marketplace needs without some investigation to verify your instincts about the needs that exist in your specific area of interest.

Conducting market research is a fancy way to describe the process of finding out what individuals and companies need and are willing to pay for. As a beginning entrepreneur you need to find out very quickly if you have developed a viable business idea because even if you are in love with your idea, if very few people need it or are willing to pay for it, you will not succeed. This does not mean that you should spend an exorbitant amount of money polling thousands of people. Instead, here are some easy-to-implement ideas for discovering what the market needs and wants:

• Once you have focused on who your target clients might be, ask potential clients the same questions (to create uniformity) one-on-one, in person, or by phone; send surveys via e-mail or on a social networking Web site or by "snail" mail. Offer respondents some kind of simple and inexpensive incentive, such as a dollar bill or a book. Encourage anonymity and candid reactions.

• Run several small brainstorming sessions, facilitated by someone other than you, to generate new business ideas.

• Run several trade shows and professional association meetings where clients and other vendors or business owners meet.

• Read trade publications for market data and trends.

The type of business you operate and the clients you serve now very likely won't be the same in a year or two. Your business will evolve over time to meet marketplace trends and your own preferences and personal needs. Joy's business is a good example. When she started her own business in her early thirties, she was recruiting entry-level salespeople for commodity businesses such as copier and telephone systems companies, and doing some sales training. Her recruiting activity guaranteed her income because she was able to bring to her own business some of her clients from the contingency agency firm she had worked for as an employee for many years. Over time, Joy began to slow down the recruiting aspect of her business and eventually stopped recruiting altogether. She made a transition into sales training for the publishing industry. More recently she has made the decision to shift away gradually from training toward giving keynote speeches.

As a sole practitioner it isn't necessary to look like a large company by calling yourself president or renting an office at a posh address. What is important is presenting a professional and credible image to your clients. Here's how:

• Use a uniform approach with your marketing materials, including your business card, brochure, social media networking profile, bio, and Web site.

• Don't print an expensive brochure initially because the services or products you provide can and will change quickly—and so will the clients you work with.

• Use a professional graphic artist to design your logo. A logo is especially important if you use your name as your company name.

• Prepare a statement that succinctly describes your business to clients and anyone who asks what you do. Your statement should briefly explain what you do and effectively describe the benefits you provide to clients: "I offer consulting services to small and medium-sized businesses to help them analyze their utility costs. I then recommend ways to reduce these costs. I guarantee a minimum cost reduction of 10 percent for any client I work with, regardless of their situation or type of business."

• Learn every aspect of running your solo practice well before hiring someone else to do it. This includes bookkeeping, Web site management, proposal writing, and marketing. When you are confident that you can handle these areas, outsource whatever you can afford so that you can focus on developing business and delivering your service or product.

• Read Alan Weiss's book *Million Dollar Consulting*. It is an excellent guide for setting fees and analyzing the profitability of your services.

• Find three to five sole practitioners to share ideas and commiserate with about your businesses.

As a sole practitioner you will continually experiment with how you handle different aspects of your business. Your goal should be to figure out which services or products reap the most satisfaction and profitability for you. Your limitation as a one-person business is that you have a finite amount of time to work, so be smart about managing your time by continually assessing how you spend it.

Purchasing a Franchise

A *franchise* can be described as an ongoing relationship between a *franchisor* (the granter of the franchise) and a *franchisee* (the person who is granted the franchise), which involves rights to products and services, a trademark identity, and business concepts, including a marketing and distribution system. In other words, as a franchisee you are investing your assets in a brand and a system.

What's the upside? A franchise can provide you with quicker start-up success, a faster way to access capital to expand your business, increased earnings, and marketing strength.

The cons? You have to invest a significant amount of capital up front, and your control of what you consider *your* business is restricted by the franchisor. Innovation isn't always possible within the structure of the franchisor's system. You also may discover that the business doesn't truly match your lifestyle or skills.

Bill Anderson owns three Mailboxes Etc. (MBE) stores in Philadelphia and southern New Jersey. Of the thirty-five hundred MBE franchises in the United States, his stores rank in the top fifty in sales. Bill is the MBE franchise representative to the franchise advisory council of the International Franchise Organization and sits on the national board as secretary. When Bill started exploring the possibility of owning his own business, he didn't plan to be a franchisee. Instead, he saw a need for a place where the average consumer could go to make copies, send packages, and pick up mail, as an alternative to the post office. He himself had used Mailboxes Etc. and loved the concept. When he decided to start this type of business after researching his entrepreneurial options, Bill concluded that owning a franchise offered the most promising opportunity.

Bill's advice to anyone thinking about buying a franchise is to "buy a business, not a job." In other words, as he puts it, if you are looking for a place to go every day where your definition of marketing is locking and unlocking the door, you'll never be successful as a franchisee.

Bill is adamant about the importance of believing in the specific product or service that a franchise offers customers rather than simply buying a franchise because you can afford it. Buying a quick oil change franchise when you know nothing about cars and hate to get your hands dirty is not a recipe for success. Neither is buying a sandwich franchise when you don't enjoy dealing with food or the public.

When Bill decided that Mailboxes Etc. was the way to go, he immediately began to develop a relationship with the local Mailboxes Etc. store owner in his hometown. Bill took him to lunch and gradually, as the owner began to trust Bill, he shared important financial information with him. The owner showed Bill his monthly royalty report, and Bill analyzed the financials, including the revenue stream, the average fixed and variable expenses, and the payroll costs.

Once Bill felt comfortable that he could satisfy his income needs as a Mailboxes Etc. franchise owner, he purchased the closest available store to his home. Today, Bill describes himself as successful and happy.

If you are seriously considering becoming a franchisee, you should be able to answer the following questions affirmatively:

1. Do you have the kind of personality that can accept running your business according to someone else's plan without feeling that it will compromise your individuality?
2. Does each of the franchises you are looking at have a readily identifiable brand name and goodwill associated with it?
3. Will the franchise you are considering be an enjoyable place to own, manage, and work day to day, possibly for years?
4. Are you prepared to spend the time doing research by calling as many franchises as you can (at least ten) and visiting as many operating units as possible?
5. Would you feel proud of the product or service you are selling?
6. Is the product or service recession-proof?
7. Is the franchisor strategically minded rather than just focused on market presence? Can he or she clearly communicate this strategy to you?
8. Have you researched the competition in your area, and do you feel comfortable with the potential market?

9. Do you understand the extent of operations assistance that is available?
10. Have you found a reputable lawyer who has experience with franchise agreements?

Buying a Business

Bizbuysell (www.bizbuysell.com) is a popular resource for potential business purchasers and business owners who are selling their businesses. The opportunities for you to buy a business are varied. The challenge is, of course, to find the right one for you.

Glen Cooper is a certified business appraiser and past president of the Maine Business Brokers' Network in Portland. He explains the key reasons to buy an existing business:

1. You will inherit an established client base.
2. You may be able to retain experienced and loyal employees.
3. More favorable financing terms are available to you as the buyer of an established business, which can include seller financing, bank financing, and even financing by vendors.
4. An existing business has an accepted product or service, which defines its market position.
5. Established sales and marketing, accounting, inventory tracking, and payroll and production systems are all in place.

If you have done your homework on the company you are thinking of buying and all these things are truly in place, you will certainly jump-start your chances for success.

There are, however, some downsides to buying an existing business:

1. The process of researching a business is tedious and taxing, especially if you aren't highly analytical or adept at financial data.

2. Finding the right business that will complement your professional experience, skills, and resources can be challenging. If you have spent your entire career in a service industry, for example, it may not make sense to consider buying a manufacturing company because of the steep learning curve involved.

3. Even with the assistance of experts such as lawyers, accountants, insurance agents, and bankers (all of which you should take advantage of), it isn't always easy to uncover any serious problems in the company you are considering buying. Here are some examples of common problems that are difficult to expose: inflated income, substantial debt, and assets that have been pledged as collateral.

4. A seller often inflates the value of equipment. Always hire an independent appraiser to assess its value. If the seller of a business tells you that another buyer is about to make an offer, don't let this rush you or distract you from making a careful decision.

5. Accounts receivable problems are a common issue for most small businesses at various times. Reviewing invoices going back at least six months to identify late payers will help you become aware of cash flow history and any credit problems.

Below are some questions that can help you decide whether buying a business is the right choice for you and what you should consider in the search process.

1. What has your professional experience included (retail, manufacturing, service, finance, high tech, etc.)?

_____

_____

_____

_____

2. How long do you want to spend searching for the right business to buy? How many hours a day or week are you willing to commit?

_____

_____

_____

_____

3. Are you willing to move or commute a long distance if necessary?

_____

_____

_____

_____

4. How involved with the management of your business do you want to be? Do you see your role as an investor only, as the person who hires the people who will run it day to day, or as the one who will step in as the hands-on leader?

_____

_____

_____

_____

5. Do you have a strong network of advisers, vendors or suppliers, and potential clients in certain industries? Who are they?

_____

_____

_____

_____

6. How large do you want your business to be?

_____

_____

_____

_____

7. Do you want a business that has had steady growth with a stable cash flow or one that has more growth potential and not as consistent a cash flow?

_____

_____

_____

_____

8. Are you interested in buying a company that needs to be turned around?

_____

_____

_____

_____

9. How much cash do you have available, including potential assets, profit sharing, stocks and bonds, and savings that you can liquidate to invest in a business?

_____

_____

_____

_____

10. Do you have contacts with bankers, venture capitalists, or angel investors (high-net-worth individuals who provide capital to a start-up or early-stage company)? Who are they?

_____

_____

_____

_____

11. How soon do you need to see profits?

_____

_____

_____

_____

While these are some guidelines to contemplate, be careful not to narrow your search too much. There are many complementary industries that you may not have thought about. For example, if you're a sports enthusiast, instead of looking only at sporting goods stores, why not consider buying a small magazine or Web site that specializes in sports?

If you don't know where you can find businesses that are for sale, here are some suggestions:

- Talk to your professional network, friends, and acquaintances.
- Seek out trusted advisers such as your attorney, accountant, banker, doctor, or dentist.
- Trade associations can be very helpful if you have narrowed your search down to the type of industry you're interested in. They all have local meetings, and many have newsletters or Web sites.
- Cold-calling owners of businesses can uncover businesses for sale that haven't yet been advertised or listed with a broker. You can find the names of companies in the yellow pages, local chamber of commerce membership lists, or simply by driving through commercial areas and writing down names.
- Read newspaper and trade publication classified advertisements.
- Search the Internet by industry or business broker. Or look at the Web sites of businesses in which you are interested.
- Use a business broker, but remember that brokers nearly always represent the seller of a business, not the buyer. A successful business broker will offer you a large selection of listings or specialize in the area you've targeted.

Remember: If the owner of a company has never sold a business before, he or she can tend to overvalue the business *and* be emotional in the process. Doing your homework thoroughly costs money and takes time but is well worth it in the long run. If you are organized in your approach, however, you may become the proud owner of an established and profitable business. Remember the number of small businesses cited at the beginning of this chapter? Twenty-seven million businesses—and all you need is one!

Creating a Partnership

Finding the right person to partner with in your own business is analogous to getting married. To be successful you want to have the same values, be compatible day to day, and accept each other's limitations while leveraging strengths. Most important, you must trust each other.

You may already have a business idea and have decided to find a partner, or you may be talking to someone about first becoming business partners and then identifying the type of business you'd like to start. Either way, you should be extremely cautious about the person you will probably spend more time with than your spouse. Some suggestions for assessing your prospective business partner are these:

- Collaborate with him or her on a project or a cross-selling effort before committing to a full-time partnership. Doing this will give you the chance to observe the other person's working style and see how he or she handles business overall.
- Have a serious discussion about each other's vision for your business. Are they in sync or worlds apart?
- Be careful about partnering with someone who is too similar to you. Be sure your prospective business partner has strengths and expertise that you don't possess, and vice versa.
- Be very sure that your partner will take the financial and legal responsibilities of starting a business seriously.
- Have a discussion about who will be in charge of each area of the company.
- Once you've decided to proceed with your partnership, write down your expectations of each other about responsibilities and tasks.
- Hire a lawyer to draft a partnership agreement for you and include in it the most important component: a mechanism for ending your partnership.

- Investigate the legal and tax implications of a general partnership, a corporation, and a limited liability corporation before deciding on the one to use for your business.

A business partnership requires constant communication and hard work; however, it can be very rewarding to have a partner who shares your dream of running a successful business.

Roadblocks and Obstacles

All potential entrepreneurs can encounter roadblocks or obstacles regardless of which route they take. You can address them, however, so that you can deal with them ahead of time.

Selling. Whether you like it or not, when you are an entrepreneur, *you are always selling*. Your perseverance at sales and your ability to sell will be one of the most critical factors in your success. "Attitudes and Behaviors That Create Small Business Success," a survey conducted by Yankelovich, a market research company, found that a dominant concern of the more than two thousand entrepreneurs questioned was attracting and keeping clients, outranking worries about staffing, paying the bills, and competition.

Unfortunately, unless you have worked in sales or have been responsible for revenue as a sales manager, the whole area of sales may be foreign to you. Whether you lack experience, have a dislike for the act of selling, or don't think it is how you should be spending your time, it is important that you overcome your specific emotional and practical obstacles and embrace the idea that as an entrepreneur you are a professional salesperson.

If necessary, you can hire a sales coach who specializes in working with small business owners, or you can take classes or workshops offered by private companies and colleges and universities. Hundreds of books have been written on the subject, many of which are geared toward the person who has never sold anything before.

If you are sure that you want to go into your own business, you should begin your education in sales. Waiting until the day you open your doors doesn't make good sense. The best way to become a good salesperson is to sell and keep selling. Start now by selling your business idea to others.

If you have both a marketing plan and sales goals (the basic components of a business plan; see "Marketing Plan" on pages 175–76) and feel passionate about your business, selling will not be as difficult as you think. Sales techniques are learned like any other technical ability, and success is a matter of using specific skills rather than a reflection of how dynamic, extroverted, and bright you are. One of the greatest challenges an entrepreneur faces is maintaining sales activity while fulfilling orders or delivering service. If you have ever taken a Sales 101 course, you know that the pipeline of prospective clients must constantly be fed. Doing this successfully requires focus and discipline above all.

Cash flow. One of the biggest worries that most people have about starting their own business is giving up a steady salary. There is also anxiety about not being able to pay their bills, both personally and professionally. This is a valid concern. In a perfect world, having twelve to eighteen months' worth of cash put away in anticipation of the ups and downs of a new business (or any business for that matter) should solve the problem. But the truth is that most people don't have the ability to save that much money and end up starting their business with a smaller financial cushion. So what's the answer? If delaying starting your business for six or eight months means you'll be able to save more money, then this is a wise strategy. If your fear about not having enough money is paralyzing you from moving forward, however, then set a goal for starting your business within a specific time frame and don't let yourself off the hook.

Most people who start a business do so with savings, credit card cash advances, loans from friends and family, and severance payments. The reality is that you will be able to invest only what you have at your disposal, and this must be an amount that is comfortable for you.

Elizabeth started her business with money from a 401(k) plan from her last employer. This provided her with a sum to pay all her expenses for four months. Most financial planners or accountants would not recommend this strategy, but it was Elizabeth's only viable option at the time. Did it create stress for her knowing that she was operating in a four-month window? Absolutely! Yet Elizabeth also knew that she could borrow money from several friends if the need arose. Her fear motivated her to hustle and drum up business quickly, which she did. She had gone through the process of budgeting every single expense and was more aware of how much it cost for her to live and work than ever before in her life.

The following are some procedures you can put in place to help your cash flow stream once you're in business:

- Offer a small discount for early or on-time payment. Most accounts payable departments are trained to treat early-payment invoices as a priority.
- Request a deposit for project work or a large contract. Be sure to have your client sign a contract stating the exact terms of their payment for your products or services.
- Ask for a monthly retainer for ongoing work. This also delivers the message to your client that you value your relationship and assures your availability.
- Arrange follow-up services or products as part of the overall package you sell to your client. Obviously, in addition to helping your cash flow, you are creating residual revenue.
- Be sure you are charging fair market fees and prices. Just because you are new in your business does not mean that you should undercut your prices. Ask your competition about their pricing and ask your clients what they pay your competition.
- Have a set of goals and a strategy in place for collecting cash, including a plan for seriously delinquent payments. Don't be afraid to use outside assistance if you need to.

Lack of a support system, resources, and feedback. As an entrepreneur, it can be very lonely not to have people and resources surrounding you when you need them the most. Even if you are running a company with employees, they won't necessarily be able to provide you with the support you'll need. This means that you should immediately find or create external opportunities to supply you with this often unfulfilled need.

Networking is necessary to your success as an entrepreneur for generating sales leads. It is also a wonderful vehicle for finding other people who are in situations like your own to compare notes with and learn from. There are many structured networking groups and associations both local and national in scope. Find out what they are by asking everyone you know which groups they belong to and which ones they find most valuable. Don't just network when business is slow or when you're feeling guilty about not doing it. Make it part of your weekly schedule.

Creating a small advisory board of people who are at various levels of experience in running their own businesses is a fabulous way to learn and share your experiences. You can schedule formal meetings or communicate more informally on an as-needed basis.

Hiring a business coach who specializes in working with start-up business owners or established business owners will provide ongoing support that you will take seriously because you are paying for it.

Involve your family in your business. You will be working much harder than you ever did before, and whether you like it or not, this will eat into your family and personal time. Asking your family for advice or a different perspective helps them feel included in your business, and often they will surprise you with some great ideas.

Blending your work and your life. There is no question that if you want to be successful in your own business, you will work harder and longer than you ever did as an employee. The time you spend with work and leisure will blur, partially because of technology that enables you to work twenty-four hours a day, but also because you can always be doing something else to take care of your business. Even if you have an attorney, an accountant, a payroll service, an assistant, and a bookkeeper, you are now wearing every single functional hat in your company. If you are not planning, you are selling; if you are not updating your Web site, you are solving a problem—and on and on.

Before you start your business, write down how much time (in hours) you spend a week or month involved with the categories below. If you are not sure, then track a typical week to find out. Next to that number write down how much time you would like to spend doing those things when you start your own business.

Work _____
Commuting to work _____
Outside interests/hobbies/sports _____
Exercise _____
Vacation _____
Family and relatives _____
Religious and spiritual activities_____
Volunteer work _____
Personal business _____
Other (add your own) _____

Refer to this list every three months to see if you have been able to maintain the balance you would like to have in your life as a new entrepreneur. Getting a new business up and running is, at least initially, a twenty-four-hour proposition, and finding "true" balance may not be possible for a while.

Step 3: Create an Action Plan

A Vision Statement for Your Business

It is extremely important to remember that success is, as the cliché goes, "in the eye of the beholder." Most likely your vision of success varies greatly from your neighbor's vision. What is important is that before you start your own business, you are able to articulate your vision—to yourself and to your family. In just a moment you'll learn how to write a business plan in which you'll include many of your specific measurable goals. While your revenue and income and the number of clients you serve are certainly important, they are only a part of how you'll define and measure your success. Developing a brief written vision statement for your business is a good way to capture your business concept. This vision is what you would like your business to become; it often includes your unique selling proposition, more commonly known as USP. Your USP is that characteristic or feature that differentiates your business from your competition.

An example of a vision statement: To be recognized nationally as a leader in presentation skills services by providing innovative training, coaching, facilitating, and consulting services to our clients.

What is your vision statement?

_____

_____

_____

_____

_____

Writing a Business Plan

Regardless of what type of business you are starting, writing a business plan is very important. This is a required document if you are seeking external financial assistance, whether you are approaching a bank, private investor, or a venture capitalist. Even if you are relying solely on your personal assets to finance your business, the process that you go through to write your plan is as valuable as the outcome itself. A business plan is a road map for your success as an entrepreneur. Software is available for you to use as a template for your business plan, and there are innumerable books you can read on the subject. These are the basic components of every plan: a company overview, executive summary, marketing plan, management plan, and financial plan.

COMPANY OVERVIEW—The company overview includes both short- and long-term projections of sales, profits, market penetration, and any other measures of progress of the success of your business. The type of business you are becoming involved with (buying a business, buying a franchise, or starting a business from scratch) and the way you plan to structure the company are also part of the company overview. With the advice of a lawyer and an accountant, you may want to become a limited liability corporation (LLC or sole proprietorship), a partnership, or an "S" or "C" corporation. The way you structure your company is important for liability and tax issues. Page 265 in the Resources guide lists books that will give you guidance in this area.

Additionally, you should list the type of taxes you'll pay as a business and as an employer, as well as all legal requirements such as licensing and local, state, and federal regulations and laws. The last two items to be included in the overview are the kinds and amount of insurance protection you'll need along with the types of advisers with whom you plan to consult.

EXECUTIVE SUMMARY—This is a brief (no more than three pages) opening description written to grab the reader's attention. It is a snapshot of your company, including the market opportunity you are pursuing, your product or service, facts and figures about your target clients, a competitive strategy, your management team (if relevant), and a financial summary. Since this is the most difficult and the most important part of your business plan to write, you should write it last.

MARKETING PLAN—The best way to describe the marketing plan is that it indicates how you'll take in money. While the word *marketing* is used, this portion of your business plan is primarily focused on selling. It outlines how you propose to sell your products or services, how you plan to bring them to the attention of prospective clients, and at what price. To write your marketing plan, ask yourself the following questions:

1. What product do you plan to make or sell, or what service do you plan to provide?
2. To whom do you hope to sell it (prospective clients), and why will they buy it?
3. How many prospective clients are there, and where are they?
4. What is your competition, and how will you capture a share of the market?
5. What prices or fees do you plan to charge, and how did you calculate them?
6. How and where will you deliver your products or services?
7. How will you promote your new business (Internet, advertising, direct selling, networking, etc.)?
8. How will you keep your clients happy (deal with complaints, provide customer service)?

MANAGEMENT PLAN—While your marketing plan describes how you'll take in money, the management plan describes how you are going to spend it as well as how you will structure and operate your business. Write your management plan using the following questions as guidelines:

1. What will you name your business? GoDaddy (www .godaddy.com) is the number one site for searching for and purchasing Internet domain names and web hosting. You can choose to register your name with the Patent and Trademark Office of the United States, which will keep your company name protected anywhere in the United States and on the Internet.
2. How will you manage your business day to day?
3. Where will you locate your business? This may be crucial

for a restaurant, for example, but not important for a sole proprietor or consultant.

4. What equipment and furniture will you need, and how much will they cost?
5. What kind of phone service and office equipment will you need, and how much will they cost?
6. Will you need materials or inventory, and who will supply them and at what price?
7. Do you plan to hire employees? What skills and qualifications will they need? How much will you pay them?
8. What records will you keep? How will you keep track of taxes, insurance, lease information, employee payroll and benefits, and so on?
9. Who will do your bookkeeping and accounting?

FINANCIAL PLAN—This translates your business into dollars and cents. It spells out how much you think it will cost to get started and operate for one or more years, how much you think you'll need to take in from sales, and how much you will need to borrow to make your entrepreneurial vision a reality.

You should detail your costs of operating for the first year or until the break-even point. This should include every item that will cost your business money: rent, utilities, taxes, salaries, employee benefits, postage, marketing costs, office supplies, and so forth. Include everything! You will develop this information by preparing a budget for your start-up year and each year thereafter.

You should present how much money you expect to take in during your first year in business or until you break even, and the total amount you will need to get started and keep your business functioning.

The amount of money you plan to invest from your own resources—savings, credit card cash advances, a severance payment, or refinancing your mortgage (home-equity loan)—and the amount you will borrow from friends and family should be listed.

If you are planning to borrow money from your bank or another outside source, it will be interested in all the information in your business plan and what your business experience and management capabilities are. It will also ask for a financial statement covering your personal assets, liabilities, and any collateral you are prepared to invest.

You can attach supporting documents such as résumés; references from creditors, potential clients, and suppliers; a lease agreement; relevant contracts; partnership agreements; and documentation of your company structure.

Even if you choose not to write a business plan when you are starting your business, it will prove to be a tremendously helpful exercise when you're thinking of expanding your business or are experiencing problems in your business or if you decide to take a more strategic approach to running your business. Obviously, it is optimum to write a business plan when starting from the ground up, but not everyone does so.

Twenty-six Things You Should Do
When Starting Your Business

As you start planning your new business, here are some of the things you should do. Please note that these suggestions are not in any order, nor are they relevant to every type of entrepreneurial venture. Check off each one as you do it.

☐ 1. Interview three entrepreneurs and ask them to share their best advice with you.

☐ 2. Identify your business niche and write a brief mission statement explaining your niche. Also known as your "two-minute drill" or your defining statement, this is different from your company vision.

☐ 3. Obtain two or three referrals to accountants. Meet and interview them.

☐ 4. Do the same for an attorney and for a Certified Financial Planner (CFP).

☐ 5. Get a long-term disability policy before you quit your job.

☐ 6. Investigate your health insurance options.

☐ 7. Name your business.

☐ 8. Decide on your business structure now. Will your business be an LLC, a "C," or an "S" corporation?

☐ 9. Get an employer identification number (EIN) for IRS purposes. Call 800-TAX-FORM or ask your accountant how to do this.

☐ 10. Get licenses and permits. Depending on your business, you can contact your city's business license department, the city zoning board, or the health department.

☐ 11. Set up a Web site.

☐ 12. List your personal assets.

☐ 13. Make a budget for your personal expenses.

☐ 14. If you need financing, get it while you are still working.

☐ 15. Find a location. If you are planning to work from home, check IRS requirements. If you need retail or commercial space, consider accessibility, proximity to competitors, taxes, insurance, utilities, and maintenance.

☐ 16. Open a business checking account.

☐ 17. Research equipment. You will need a computer, printer, scanner, modem, DSL or cable line, copier, phone, postage meter, and cell phone or pager, among other things.

☐ 18. Be sure you have technical support lined up for all your equipment.

☐ 19. Find a graphic artist to design your logo, business cards, and stationery, and get them printed.

☐ 20. Find suppliers through trade shows, buyers' directories, trade publications, business-to-business yellow pages, and referrals.

☐ 21. Get merchant credit card status. American Express and Discover can be contacted directly. Visa and MasterCard accounts are established through your bank.

☐ 22. Create a credit application for customers.

☐ 23. Advertise job openings on the Internet.

□ 24. Create a job application, making sure it meets legal guidelines.

□ 25. Get relevant business insurance, such as workers' compensation, liability, property/casualty, and automobile.

□ 26. Start networking and generating business.

The beauty of starting your own business is that it's yours to do with what you want. As an entrepreneur you'll have your unique fingerprint on your business. Here are two success stories to illustrate the point.

After twenty-eight years in information technology, Harry wanted more meaning and balance as well as "to live more fully." He decided to start a personal and business coaching company, which he named All About Enterprises. When asked if he was satisfied with his new business, he replied, "Very satisfied! My new business is tied to my core values (by design!). I really like the idea of more flexibility and control of my time and focus. I believe that I can build upon my fifteen years of consulting to build my own coaching/training practice."

After eleven years with Citibank, Sheri resigned from her position as a vice president and started a business, Cotton Candy Kids, which designs and creates custom children's accessories. Sheri expresses well what so many entrepreneurs feel: "Cotton Candy Kids is a perfect blend for me at this time in my life. It allows me to stay home with my children, put my creative 'juices' to work, have a sense of accomplishment, meet new people, and keep the brain working! I have always loved sewing and needed a creative outlet. Someone once told me, 'When you do what you love for a living, it's as easy as breathing.' The business has really taken off, and the path has felt as natural as breathing. It rejuvenates my mind and soul."

The process of starting a business can be overwhelming, and you will find very quickly that some entrepreneurial options are a better fit for you than others. Once you have identified the one or two options you'd like to explore, do the first thing on the list of twenty-six suggestions you just read: Find several people who are doing what you think you'd like to do and talk to them about their experience and recommendations they have for you to get started.

CHAPTER 10

One Toe in the Retirement Pool

The American Association of Retired Persons (AARP), the powerful advocacy group for people older than fifty, reported that 79 percent of baby boomers said they don't plan to stop working at age sixty-five, creating a "working retirement" for both personal and financial reasons. In the dictionary, retirement is defined as "going away from business or public life" or "concluding one's working or professional life."

Today, age is not necessarily an indicator that you should retire. Someone who retires at age sixty-five could have twenty or twenty-five years left to live. According to the U.S. Census Bureau, the sixty-five-and-older segment of the population will increase to 72 million in 2030. A good percentage of these people will still want to work—doing what they had done previously or becoming involved in something that will be different, but they will still work.

If you are eyeing "retirement" in the next several years, are about to retire now, or have already retired and still want to work in some way, the first step is to think long and hard about why you are considering retirement. Among your reasons may be the following:

1. You are simply ready to retire. You have thought about it for a while, and although you aren't necessarily sure about what you'll do when you retire, you know that it's time. You have tired of the grind of working or have had numerous unhappy job situations and just don't want to participate in the battle that work can be at times.

John, at fifty-six, manages a worldwide business for a health-care company in the areas of clinical diagnostics and marketing and has worked since he was sixteen and a half. He just isn't interested in working anymore. He thinks about retirement constantly and believes that many of his peers are doing so as well.

2. Your spouse or significant other is in the same stage of life as you and is also ready to retire or has done so recently. While it isn't necessary to retire side by side with your partner, the adjustment period that goes along with not working full-time and changing your lifestyle is easier to go through with someone else. Surrounding yourself with friends, former colleagues, relatives, and peers to socialize with and count on as a support group makes retirement so much more pleasurable. If you know enough people who are in the same phase of life that you are, retiring can be even more attractive.

3. You want to retire while you're still in good health so that you can fully enjoy your retirement years. Even if you are in good physical shape now, you may experience health problems as a result of normal aging, some of which you won't be able to anticipate or control. On the other hand, if you are not as healthy as you used to be, retirement is less stressful than working full-time. As the saying goes, "If you don't have your health, you don't have anything."

4. You are reasonably comfortable with the financial aspects of retirement. Income and finances are usually the first thing that people focus on when thinking about taking this step—not surprisingly, since these are also the topics that cause the most concern. Many people do not have a company pension plan, and many

others have experienced unforeseen financial reversals in their lives, such as failed investments, shifts in the stock market, or huge uninsured medical expenses. The majority of people retiring will suffer a drop in income no matter what their situation is. While John fantasizes about retiring, he knows that in order to live the lifestyle he and his wife desire, he can't realistically retire until he's sixty-two. "Having enough to live on with what we have stored away" is his serious concern. He is willing to "hang in there" for another six years in order to ensure that this will happen.

5. Family issues such as caring for your elderly parents and spending more time with your grandchildren have become more important. While the focus of this chapter is on older individuals, this category also includes those who aren't necessarily older but have found it too difficult to effectively manage both a career and a family. Keri, only thirty-four, loved her career as a vice president of recruiting for an investment bank but has decided to "retire" to spend time with her children and husband. "I found a lot of satisfaction in managing a career and love my time now with my family. I'd like to try to have both but am not sure I can do it and feel satisfied or competent at both."

6. You have a lot of hobbies and interests you yearn to become more involved with, or you'd like to develop certain skills or expertise that you haven't taken the time to do while working.

Several or all of these reasons can significantly influence why, when, and how you choose to retire. Take some time to think about each one and decide its relevance to your specific situation.

Step 1: Complete the "One Toe in the Retirement Pool" Self-Assessment

Retiring from your full-time career will enable you to be flexible about the kind of work you'll do and how you'll do it, giving you the opportunity to explore interests, hobbies, or another kind of work.

Review your top ten values on page 33 to remind yourself of what's important to you.

Next, review the interests and favorite skills you wrote down on pages 51 and 58–59, as they will provide the foundation for the type of work you'll find or create. Are there several interests you'd like to get involved with when you retire? Write them down below.

_____

_____

_____

_____

Now do the same for your favorite skills. List the ones that you would like to use for the first time or continue using once you've created your retired life.

_____

_____

_____

_____

Now, keeping your self-assessment results in mind, ask yourself, "If I could do any work in the world after I 'retire,' what would it be? Where would I do it? With whom would I be doing it?"

_____

_____

_____

_____

_____

Once you have refamiliarized yourself with the results of your self-assessment, it's time to do some thinking and exploring about your retirement.

Answering these simple questions can help you ascertain the additional soul-searching and research you need to do to help you plan for retirement:

1. Have you always thought you'd retire at a certain age? If so, what is it?

   _____

   _____

   _____

2. What are or were your reasons for picking this age?

   _____

   _____

   _____

3. Have you already met with a financial planner to plan for retirement?

   _____

   _____

   _____

4. If not, why haven't you?

   _____

   _____

   _____

5. Do you have an up-to-date will, a revocable trust, and appropriate insurance coverage for you and your family?

_____

_____

_____

6. How do you feel about retiring? Have you really sat down and thought through the possible positive and negative implications of it?

_____

_____

_____

7. Can you picture what retirement would look like for you from a lifestyle standpoint (where you'll live, your proximity to your family, etc.)?

_____

_____

_____

8. Have you had a serious discussion with your spouse and immediate family about retiring?

_____

_____

_____

9. If so, what are their concerns about it?

_____

_____

_____

10. If not, when do you plan to do so?

_____

_____

_____

11. Do you know others who have retired within the last several
    years? If so, have you had an earnest conversation with them
    about what they've experienced so far?

_____

_____

_____

Retirement as we've known it is being transformed into a different type of transition phase. You must prepare yourself emotionally, psychologically, and financially for this new phase, whether it
means you're working or not. To do so you must talk to people,
research, and be very thoughtful about who you are. You must
know what your goals are in life and what makes you happy as well
as fulfilled. Nowadays it is quite likely that you will live a very
long time after you "retire."

Step 2: Exploring Roadblocks and Opportunities

Your Finances

A 2009 survey by Gallup revealed that 52 percent of Americans say that they won't have enough money when they retire.

Your retirement income will be financed by any investments you may have, Social Security, pension plans, real estate, and income you generate from working. You may not have all these sources of income when you retire, particularly given the recent stock market dive, so planning how much you will have is very important.

Phased retirement plans will become more and more prevalent as time goes on. These allow older workers to leave a company gradually over a period of five years or so. The employer distributes the worker's pension withdrawal, compensation, and medical benefits incrementally over time. In a 2008 survey by Hewitt Associates, 21 percent of employers considered phased retirement critical to their company's HR strategy, but this tripled to 61 percent when they looked ahead five years.

The sad truth is that many people who retire depend almost solely on Social Security for income, despite the fact that it was never intended to provide 100 percent of a retiree's income. In fact, in 2009, according to the Social Security Administration, 10.6 million people, or 22 percent of the 48 million who receive Social Security, live on that check alone. According to Mike Robbins, author of *Smart Guide to Planning for Retirement*, the Social Security program is currently designed to replace about 42 percent of the "average" retiree's preretirement income. On top of this dismal reality, Social Security has been in trouble for a long time, and the future looks bleak unless the entire system is overhauled. According to the Social Security Administration, by 2011, when the first baby boomers hit the official retirement age of sixty-five, the ratio of workers to retirees will be somewhere between 2.5 to 1. When the program began in 1935, this ratio was fifty workers to every one retiree. This is a significant statistic because the people who are working are the ones who continue to fund Social Security. Mike Robbins advises that when calculating the retirement income you'll need, you should factor in a longer-than-usual life span, inflation, and the fact that your money will keep working for you while you are retired.

One way to ease your financial worries for retirement is to hire a financial planner. When you are selecting a financial planner, use the following criteria:

1. Is the person as interested in your values, lifestyle, and goals as he or she is in your financial situation?
2. Is he or she approachable, empathetic, and a good listener?
3. Does the person have a definite philosophy about building wealth?
4. Is the person willing to share his or her personal portfolio with you? In other words, does the person do for him- or herself what he or she advises others to do?
5. Does the person have specific experience with individuals planning retirement? What has his or her track record been with these clients? Can you interview a few of them?

Whether you use a financial planner or do the numbers on your own, you may find—depending on your situation, the economy, and shifting societal attitudes—that you need to keep working longer than you had hoped. John, the health-care executive, is a good example of this. He has another six years to retirement and believes that planning for retirement is "like a chess game. It's important to position properly all the pieces of retirement—your 401(k), your pension if you have one, your IRA, medical insurance, your investments, and all the other financial tools that are relevant to your well-being." He goes on to say, "The other important part of thinking about retiring is 'where.' Where do you want to live?"

Choosing Where to Live When You're Retired

In *Retirement on a Shoestring*, John Howells recommends places to retire, ranging from Mexico and Costa Rica to Oklahoma and Mississippi. Since his targeted readership is those people who must get by in retirement solely on Social Security, Howells is more focused on the cost of living than on other lifestyle issues, such as community services and culture.

While a lower cost of living is important to many retirees, other reasons to move to a different state are for a better climate, community services geared toward the elderly, medical care, an easier lifestyle, and a greater availability of property and land. The U.S. Census Bureau has projected that by the year 2020, Nevada, Arizona, Colorado, Utah, Washington, Georgia, Alaska, and California will double their older populations, for many of these reasons.

If you are considering moving to a different state, region, or another country, be sure to visit for a week and talk to some of the residents, including people who have moved there to retire. Here are some things you should look for when you're exploring a new geographic area to live:

- *Climate.* While warm weather may be appealing, can you handle suffocating summers?
- *Taxes.* What are the property, state income, and sales taxes?
- *Housing.* Are there houses that are appealing to you? Rental communities? Continuing-care housing? Shared housing?
- *Medical care.* Is there an adequate hospital? Are there enough doctors to take care of the community? Do you have a special health problem that can be monitored and taken care of?
- *Transportation.* Are there taxis and buses, and is there easy accessibility to the closest airport?
- *Proximity to your family and friends.* Is it easy to visit you? Is it a place that people will find appealing to visit?
- *Culture.* Are there museums, a theater, a symphony? Are there libraries close by?

- *Social interactions.* Are there people in the community with similar cultural backgrounds or interests to whom you can relate?
- *Services for the elderly.* What kinds of community services exist for the aging?
- *Education.* Are there colleges or universities nearby where you can take classes?
- *Your interests.* Is this an area where you can involve yourself in your particular interest, such as art, music, fishing, hunting, skiing, tennis, or golf?
- *Industry.* What kinds of businesses exist? Are there companies where you can work full-time or part-time?
- *Safety.* Is the crime rate low? Will you feel comfortable walking or driving around the area?
- *Affordability.* How much do food, gas, utilities, movie tickets, and clothing cost? How much does it cost to eat in a restaurant? What is the overall cost of living?

What Kind of Work Do You
Want to Do in Retirement?

The Futurist magazine predicts that "increasingly, over time, people will work at one career, 'retire' for a while when they can afford it, return to school, begin another career, and so on in endless variations. True retirement, a permanent end to work, will be delayed until very late in an extended life." Indeed, you may be part of the growing trend of older workers who are staying in the workforce. In some ways you are not unlike many of the people who fit into the other five situations in this book. Whether you are wondering Where's the Meaning? or are Bored and Plateaued, the first thing you must do is get reacquainted with yourself so that you can focus your goals and energy in the appropriate direction.

Michael did just this when he retired at age sixty-five and moved from New York City to Cape Cod, where he had owned a home for years. He started helping a local florist part-time and now works three or four days a week delivering flowers. He tells stories about the times he rings someone's doorbell and the person opens the door to see Michael standing there with a bouquet of flowers. It gives him joy to see the delighted expression on that individual's face. He helps many elderly recipients of flowers find a vase, keeping them company for a few minutes. Michael, who worked as an executive in the outplacement business for many years, frankly never expected to get so much pleasure out of a task like delivering flowers, but he always knew that having meaning in his work was important.

Have you always wanted to start your own business? Maybe you didn't think you could afford to or weren't willing to make the sacrifices when you were in your peak working years. Lee was reorganized out of a twenty-five-year career and at fifty-seven, as he is eyeing retirement, he is on his own as a broker of award products for the incentive industry. He loves the independence and plans on dabbling in this business even when he slows down his work schedule.

Ernie enjoyed a very satisfying career as a product sales manager for a large chemical company. Over sixty, he officially retired from his job and immediately began pursuing opportunities to become a speaker with an emphasis on selling. In the beginning stages of his exploration of the speaking business, Ernie hired a coach to help him create a one-hour speech. Then he began learning more about the craft of speaking by joining Toastmasters (a national association that focuses on teaching people to speak) and several speakers' associations. He also started networking with his contacts in the chemical business to learn about possible speaking opportunities. While Ernie is excited about this new part-time "career," he also is adamant that his "basic thrust is to work at a level that will keep me interested and challenged, with the money being a secondary consideration."

What about simply working to fulfill some of your social needs or your desire to be useful, or to supplement your income? In a *Parade* magazine article, "Retire from Life? Never!" Neal Cole, eighty, tells a story of his work at Portland International Airport in Oregon doing security check-ins and pushing wheelchairs for travelers in need. He makes $6.50 an hour and another $15 or $20 a day in tips. As he says, "I get to talk to a lot of people, and I've lost forty pounds."

Zetta is ninety-two and works at the Top of the Falls souvenir shop in Niagara Falls, New York, during the peak tourist season, April to October. She had never had a steady career, opting instead to raise her three children full-time. On occasion she had worked as a jewelry engraver, an independent salesperson, a bank teller, and a clerical assistant. After not working for thirty years, Zetta took a job in the gift shop and has worked there for twenty years. She explains that while she never gets bored while home alone, she does get lonely, and now she enjoys her interaction with the tourists. Zetta admits that if she didn't have to show up for work, she wouldn't stay active. The best part? "I love meeting people. Sometimes I make an instant connection with someone, and even if I know I will never see the person again, I feel as if I have a friend for life." Zetta teaches herself German, using audiotapes and videotapes, and has fun trying to talk to the many German-speaking tourists who visit Niagara Falls. She makes $8.25 an hour, which supplements her Social Security. While the small amount of money helps, the other benefits far outweigh the financial ones.

Corporations are learning that retaining, retraining, and hiring older workers is a smart business strategy. In an era in which the ability to find workers with the right skills has become more difficult for companies, the older worker is often the solution to this problem. In addition to the marketplace's need for talented labor and a greater availability of people in older age groups, there are other reasons that make it sensible to hire older workers:

• Bringing back people who had worked at a corporation previously helps preserve the corporate memory, a crucial component of a corporate culture.

• Rapid changes in the job market and technology have necessitated the need for additional education and retraining for every level of employee. More and more, even small companies see this as a necessary investment rather than an expense. Also, the traditional bias toward training only new employees or senior managers appears to be diminishing. This creates a willingness to hire the older worker and to train him or her alongside everyone else.

• A *New York Times* article cited the results of a Harris poll that asked 774 corporate human resources directors about older workers. Of those interviewed, 80 percent agreed that older workers (age fifty-five and up) had less turnover, and 71 percent said these workers had as much ability as younger employees to acquire new skills. Yet, according to AARP data, while work ethic, loyalty, and experience rank high on employer surveys about the traits possessed by older workers, inflexibility and a lack of technical skills are cited as being the downside to these employees.

Melanie has had a successful career as an insurance underwriter and loved the technical aspects of her work, and, like many of us, Melanie has suffered through many less than enjoyable work situations. A year or so after her husband retired, Melanie found herself in yet another difficult and stressful work environment and decided to retire to keep her husband company as well as to restore her psychological well-being. She stopped working, traveled, read, and caught up on projects she hadn't been able to do while working. The first year or so was great, but Melanie, only in her early fifties, began to feel antsy. While she did retire at an earlier age than most people do, she feels that if she had put more time into planning her retirement, she would have experienced more satisfaction. She went back to work, but in a job that was at a much lower level than any of her previous positions, and while the challenge and the status no longer existed, the long hours and demands on her were still there. On top of this, her compensation was much reduced from her previous employment as an underwriter. She eventually left that job and at fifty-five took a job comparable to the one she had left before she retired. She plans to retire again at fifty-nine and a half, but this time she says her approach will be different. She will spend more time preparing herself mentally and will organize her affairs before she actually retires. Her advice? "Take the time to plan your retirement. It should be approached just like a job search. If you don't, you may be shocked by what you'll experience when you retire."

Step 3: Create an Action Plan

It is nice to know that as you are approaching retirement, you have a wide array of options available to you. Whether you are "chomping at the bit" to retire and never work again (15 percent of people planning retirement don't want to work at all) or excited about starting a second part-time career, there are some things you should think about and do before you take the plunge. Examine the details of your life as if you are doing "due diligence" to buy a business:

• All of the many financial details that are so important to your retirement should be scrutinized and analyzed by you and by experts. As Mike Robbins says in his book *Smart Guide to Planning for Retirement*, "Retirement is the single largest financial goal most of us face."

• Defer any retirement income you have as long as you can to reap the maximum benefits.

• If you can, wait as long as possible to collect your Social Security benefits so that you will receive the maximum amount for which you are eligible. David waited until he was seventy to retire and as a result receives $2,000 a month from Social Security.

• Allow yourself to dream about the different work opportunities you can explore. Whether you want to start a business, hang out a consulting shingle, or work part-time for a company, you can believe that anything is possible. Does the world discriminate against older people in the workforce? Of course. Your objective, however, is to find that niche for yourself where discrimination won't affect you.

• Do much of the legwork and planning for your new work venture *before* you retire. Give yourself a reasonable amount of time to learn about what you need to know and do.

• Check out www.2young2retire.com for ideas about reinventing retirement for yourself. This site offers tips, tools, and stories about how to gain a fresh perspective on your "postcareer" life, whether it be a new career or business, volunteer or nonprofit work, going back to school, or learning something new.

• Get a clean bill of health. Make appointments with all your doctors, including your internist, dentist, dermatologist, gynecologist, and any other specialists.

Use the following questions to plan your retirement:

1. Do you have a financial planner with whom you feel comfortable?

_____

_____

_____

2. If not, when will you begin getting referrals and interviewing financial planners?

_____

_____

_____

3. Are there geographic locations that you are interested in relocating to? What are they?

_____

_____

_____

4. Have you investigated them thoroughly? If not, when do you plan to do so?

_____

_____

_____

5. If you are working now, when do you plan to leave your job?

_____

_____

_____

6. Have you thought about the kind of work you'd like to do when you leave your current position? If so, what is it?

_____

_____

_____

7. What steps do you plan on taking to create new work or find your next job?

_____

Remember that this next phase in your life should be fun, interesting, fulfilling, illuminating, and exhilarating! In an article written by Lydia Bronte, a senior fellow at the Hunter College Brookdale Center on Aging commented, "Some people find their best fit career-wise after the age of fifty and some, even more surprisingly, after the age of sixty-five. People need to keep in mind that the best part of your career may still be ahead of you."

Jerry is a great example of this. After working in multiple careers that included the Navy, consumer product sales, executive search and outplacement, Jerry, at sixty-eight, is retired from the corporate world. He started his own small company, which provides career transition seminars for flag rank military (admirals and generals), counseling and retention classes at the Naval War College in Newport, Rhode Island, and other career management services for junior naval officers. He feels so blessed that at the end of a series of successful careers, he has been able to create work for himself that he loves and excels at. Jerry says, "I feel that my background in management as well as the need to 'do good' have prepared me for the work I'm doing, which has real meaning. I'm away from corporate politics, although I miss the social interaction. As long as God gives me the health and the credibility, I plan on continuing to contribute as long as possible, perhaps ratcheting down a bit at a time. This year I'll work about ten percent less than last year, but I get paid real well for what I do, and I have a modest Navy Reserve retirement and also now collect Social Security."

Len, sixty-five, sold his bread distribution business when he was sixty-two. An avid fisherman and hunter, he wanted a flexible schedule, so he went to work for a limousine service in central Florida, where he drives people to and from the airport. While he enjoys meeting new people every day, he's beginning to feel that his employer is too dependent on him. Because of this, Len has decided to find another type of part-time work. He loves the fact that he can keep trying different kinds of work, something he couldn't do easily when he was supporting his family by working in his own business.

Retirement can and should be an interesting and fulfilling phase in your life. It is an ideal time to experiment with different kinds of work without the stress and pressures that you may have experienced in your career. As a recent AARP ad says, "Age is just a number, and life is what you make of it."

CHAPTER 11

The Eleven Keys to Success

In his best-selling book *Emotional Intelligence*, Daniel Goleman writes, "There are widespread exceptions to the rule that IQ predicts success—at best, IQ contributes about 20 percent to the factors that determine life success, which leaves 80 percent to other forces." Goleman goes on to explain, "These other characteristics are called emotional intelligence: abilities such as being able to motivate oneself and persist in the face of frustrations; to control impulse and delay gratification; to regulate one's moods and keep distress from swamping the ability to think; to empathize and to hope."

This book is full of assessments, tools, resources, and how-tos to help guide you in finding new work that will better meet your personal and financial needs. No matter which category you fit within, however, unless you are able to demonstrate and master a very specific set of life skills and traits, you will find it very difficult to be successful in finding the work you want.

"The Eleven Keys to Success" come from intuitive observations of and experience with people in the workplace. Time and again it is apparent that those individuals who exhibit these eleven keys and use them most productively are consistently the more successful and well-liked individuals overall. The good news is that most people are born with at least some of these keys or learned them at a very young age, and all of these keys can be developed or learned later in life.

These are the Eleven Keys to Success:

1. **Confidence:** an unshakable belief in oneself based on a realistic understanding of one's circumstances; a trait that most people admire in others and strive to acquire themselves.

2. **Curiosity:** being eager to know and learn; always showing interest and giving special attention to the less obvious; always being the person who says, "I want to know more about. . . ."

3. **Decisiveness:** arriving at a final conclusion or making a choice and taking action; making decisions with determination even when you don't have all the information you think you need.

4. **Empathy:** demonstrating caring and understanding of someone else's situation, feelings, and motives; always thinking about what it's like to walk in someone else's shoes.

5. **Flexibility:** being capable of change; responding positively to change; being pliable, adaptable, non-rigid, and able to deal with ambiguity.

6. **Humor:** viewing yourself and the world with enjoyment; not taking life or yourself too seriously; being amusing, amused, and, at times, even comical.

7. **Intelligence:** thinking and working smartly and cleverly; being sharp in your dealings; "not reinventing the wheel"; planning before acting; working efficiently and focusing on quality over quantity. (Important note: This is different from IQ, the common abbreviation for intelligence quotient.)

8. **Optimism:** expecting the best possible outcome and dwelling on the most hopeful or positive aspects of a situation;

subscribing to the belief that "the glass is half full" rather than "half empty."

9. **Perseverance:** having passion, energy, focus, and the desire to get results. Motivation, persistence, and hard work are all aspects of Perseverance.

10. **Respect:** remembering that it is just as easy to be nice; protecting another person's self-esteem; treating others in a considerate and courteous manner.

11. **Self-awareness:** a sophisticated form of consciousness that enables you to regulate yourself by self-monitoring, observing yourself, and changing your thought processes and behaviors.

Which of these keys are among your strengths? Which of the eleven are among your weaknesses? Self-awareness, the eleventh key, is really the foundation for understanding yourself. If you are not sure how self-aware you are, ask several people whom you trust which of these eleven keys they believe are your strengths and which are not. Again, while no one person possesses all ten of these keys in equal amounts, each of them can be developed and improved.

Confidence

Self-confidence—an unshakable belief in oneself based on a realistic understanding of one's circumstances—is a trait that most people admire in others and strive to acquire themselves. Confident people exude positive energy that draws others to them like a magnet. They tend to be optimists and risk-takers, and they excel at working under pressure, tolerating frustration, and coping with adversity. Confident individuals usually appear calm, relaxed, and "comfortable in their own skin." These are the people we all want to work with because their confidence is inspiring and becomes contagious.

It is important to possess a healthy level of confidence in order to change your career, start a business, or look for a job. A large part of the process for any of these changes seems ambiguous and uncertain; therefore, keeping your perspective at a realistic level is a must!

Assess Your Confidence

Take the following assessment to help you decide whether you lack confidence, have too much confidence, or have just the right amount.

Indicate how true each statement is for you by placing the appropriate number in the blank to the left of the statement.

5 = Definitely true

4 = Often true

3 = Somewhat true

2 = Rarely true

1 = Almost never true

____1. I really like and accept who I am.

____2. Usually I do not take mistakes or setbacks personally and can view them as learning experiences.

____3. I never spend time thinking about how I can avoid looking bad or being embarrassed.

____4. I believe that I deserve the best that life has to offer.

____5. I can easily make a list of eight accomplishments in my work and personal life in the last five years.

____6. I express my opinions and feelings openly.

____7. I really trust my intuition or "gut" and follow what it tells me.

____8. I am able to visualize what I want or need and make it happen.

_____ 9. I feel proud of myself when I overcome obstacles or improve something about myself.

_____10. I am always conscious of how important my image (that is, demeanor, appearance, the way you act and communicate) is.

_____11. I accept compliments graciously and without discomfort.

_____12. I enjoy feeling successful.

_____13. I have no trouble saying no to other people when I need to.

_____14. I don't believe that others' perceptions of me are more accurate than my own.

_____15. I do not need to be liked by everyone in my life at all times.

_____16. My past does not influence my behavior and feelings.

_____17. I don't often magnify the negative aspects of things.

_____18. My behavior almost always reflects the way I feel inside.

SCORE KEY

Add up the numbers that you entered for each question. If you scored:

18 to 35	Your low self-confidence is probably negatively affecting many aspects of your life. It may make sense to seek professional counseling to understand why your self-assurance is so low.
36 to 54	You probably feel confidence in some areas of your life and less confidence in others. While this is normal for many people, it could benefit you to focus on increasing your confidence in those areas that can use it.
55 to 72	You like and respect yourself and have learned to accept both your positive and negative qualities. Because you feel good about yourself, you tend to enjoy life.

73 to 90   You may be too confident at times and not have
                    a realistic outlook of yourself. People could view
                    you as egotistical or conceited at times. It is pos-
                    sible that you aren't actually that confident but
                    cover it up by acting overly confident.

If your score fell between 55 and 72 and you feel comfortable
with your level of confidence, you may want to focus on how to
deal with other people who are either too confident or are not confident enough.

If you scored lower than you would like or fell into the too-
confident category, the following assessments will help you pin-
point some reasons and the behaviors you exhibit.

If you would like to boost your confidence, try one of the following exercises:

Give Yourself Credit for Past Effort and Successes

Write down two positive things that you have achieved in the last
six months. Have you learned something new? Have you started
an exercise program or lost weight? Have you solved a problem
that had been bugging you?

_____

_____

_____

_____

Now think about what you did to make your accomplishment
happen. Did you adjust your attitude? Did you write down your
goal and look at it frequently? Did you take a class, read a book,
or ask someone for help?

_____

_____

_____

_____

The purpose of this exercise is to remind you that you have recently been successful in making something good happen for yourself, and if you've done it before, you can do it again. Applauding yourself for achieving something meaningful or desirable to you, no matter how simple, is a great technique for developing confidence.

Create a Positive "Incantation"

If you lack confidence, you may have a habit of using negative "self-talk," unflattering or overly critical words that you say to yourself either silently or out loud and that only make you feel less confident. An incantation is a simple phrase or group of words recited to produce a magical effect. In this case the desired magical effect is bolstering your self-image. To help create your incantation, write down something negative that you habitually say about yourself, either out loud or silently. Here's an example: Whenever Gwen forgets to ask her boss a question, she always tells herself, "I did something really stupid." If Gwen took time to think about it logically, she would realize that the idea of labeling herself "stupid" just because she didn't get all the information she needs from her boss is, well, ridiculous!

_____

_____

_____

_____

Now think of a positive phrase or motivating expression that has meaning to you and write it down. In Gwen's case she might write, "Create an opportunity to connect." The next time Gwen forgets to ask her boss something, she can say to herself, "I just created another opportunity to connect with my boss!"

_____

_____

_____

_____

The next time you catch yourself using negative self-talk, quickly substitute the incantation you've just written down. Doing this repeatedly will help you develop belief in yourself, and create a new habit of positive "self-talk." Gradually, this new habit will replace your old one and help you strengthen your faith in yourself.

Take a Risk

People with low confidence tend to shy away from undertaking new experiences because of their fear of failure. Learning to approach new experiences as opportunities to learn new things, rather than occasions to win or lose, is the key to positive risk taking. Think of something at work you'd like to do, something that you see as risky (which has prevented you from doing it). Do you want to network with a senior executive in your company? Do you want to volunteer for a task force? Do you want to make a presentation at an upcoming meeting? Whatever it is, write it down.

_____

_____

_____

_____

Write down, step-by-step, what you have to do to make that thing you're itching to do—but are afraid of—happen. Try to keep it simple. Do you need to learn more about the thing you have in mind? Who do you need to talk with? What kind of preparation do you need to do? What about taking a class?

_____

_____

_____

_____

Now that you've named the risky thing you'd like to do and the steps needed to accomplish it, write down the three worst things that might happen if you take a risk and fail to achieve the results you were hoping for.

_____

_____

_____

_____

Realistically, what are the chances of each one of these things happening? If it did happen, how would you, or someone you care about, be affected? Now look at your answers and try to honestly determine how much they are based on your fear or on a logical assessment of the situation.

What Do You Like About Yourself?

Make a list of five things you like about yourself. Don't ask anyone else what he or she likes about you. Make this list on your own.

_____

_____

_____

_____

What Do Other People Like About You?

Ask five people to tell you one thing that they like about you. If someone repeats an answer you've already received, ask for a different answer. Write the answers down.

_____

_____

_____

_____

Are any of the answers the same as yours? If so, that's great because it confirms that what you already know about yourself is what others value about you as well. Now write the entire list on an index card or put it into your PDA device. Whenever you are feeling less confident, go to a place where you have some privacy, pull out your list, and read it aloud!

Healthy confidence is one of the most valuable assets you can have in life and in a job search or career change. Of the Eleven Keys, Confidence is one of the hardest keys to learn and maintain, but without it the other keys can't be learned as easily.

Curiosity

Are you curious? Do you constantly seek to learn about new ideas and gather new information, no matter what the topic? Or are you concerned only with learning about and knowing just what interests you? When you meet a new person, do you really make an effort to get to know him or her, or are many of your encounters superficial in nature?

We all have an unlimited potential for learning. We can also hold ourselves back from learning by allowing certain fears, such as a fear of failure or a fear of success, to inhibit us. Sometimes we let a lack of training or experience keep us from being inquisitive and interested in new things. The trouble with this approach is that being curious and learning about people, jobs, and business are extremely necessary to the process of finding satisfying work. Our natural tendency is to believe that we must be interested in something before we are willing to learn more about it. Yet at times we surprise ourselves by becoming interested in something we didn't think we cared about.

Jonathan had the courage to leave a secure job at a Fortune 50 company in order to seek a more rewarding and challenging career and to balance his family life, which included his newborn daughter. He hired a career counselor who helped him define his unique strengths, skills, passions, and hidden talents. He honed his curiosity by networking in new areas of business, attending trade shows, and exploring areas he had never been exposed to directly. Jonathan read new books, listened to audiocassettes, and attended presentations about career change. All of the new information he absorbed really opened his eyes to the career possibilities that existed for him. He started his own company doing business strategy and due diligence, and he leads a very balanced life that includes participating in his daughter's life and spending time on his boat, things he would never be able to do if he still worked for the Fortune 50 company.

When you are curious and interested in learning from others, it shows. Constantly asking questions of the people you meet and really listening to their answers during the process of exploring new career situations and opportunities—as well as in your other social interactions, both formal and informal—are great ways to develop your curiosity. Becoming a better listener will help you become more curious and interested. Really focusing intently on what people are saying, without jumping to immediate conclusions, will enable you to learn and understand information more easily. Trying to understand and learn about people's motives, feelings, and emotions—not just facts—is important as well.

Decisiveness

Making decisions is a crucial part of changing your work. One of the reasons so many people remain in an unhappy or unsatisfying job situation is that they simply can't make any decisions. The trouble with this is that without decisions there are no results! Decisions are based on gathering as much information as possible without getting stuck in a state of "analysis paralysis." Involving the people who are affected by your decisions, such as your advisers or your family, is also a meaningful part of making decisions. Your intuition—that is, what your "gut," "inner voice," or "sixth sense" tells you to do—is another significant element of decision-making. Balancing these three components can be a challenge, and making a decision, let alone making the one that's best for you, is often not that simple.

It is also very important to remember that there is no perfect decision. Deciding finally to do something about being unhappy with your work is one of the hardest decisions you can make in life. But once you have done so, continuing to make small decisions along the way will not only become easier but will help you feel better.

If you can't make a decision easily, ask yourself what the worst possible outcome could be. Rarely does the worst possible scenario ever happen, but even if it does, ask yourself what you would do if it did and how you could turn it around.

How can you be more decisive? If you follow this simple

thought process when making a decision, it will become much easier:

1. Define a specific problem or situation with your work. Try to focus on the actual problem, not the symptoms.
2. Decide what it is that you want to achieve. In other words, what do you want the immediate outcome of your decision to be? What about the long-term outcome?
3. Consider your options.
4. Do you have all the information you need to make the decision? If not, and the information is accessible, obtaining the information will make the decision a lot easier for you. You can use the formula that journalists use by asking yourself: Who? What? Where? When? Why? How? If you have all this information, there should be no reason not to make the decision.
5. Do you have to make this decision alone? While so much of the process of finding satisfying work comes from you, there is no need to do it alone. Consult with people who are supportive of you and those who are experts or at least knowledgeable about you and your situation.
6. How have you handled similar issues in the past? If you haven't had to make decisions related to your career in the past, find out how other people have done so. It is time to learn how to make this an easier and more comfortable process.
7. Do you have a track record of making poor decisions? If so, why? Is there something you can change about how you make decisions?
8. Do you rely too heavily on other people's input? Everyone has an opinion, whether you ask for it or not. Sift through this information and use what makes sense for you.
9. Is there someone whose style of decision-making you admire? Are you able to spend some time with that person to learn how he or she makes decisions?

10. If you had to decide quickly, what would your immediate decision be about what to do next regarding your
career?

In making decisions, be willing to take risks and to forgive
yourself if you make a decision that doesn't turn out to be the right
one for you.

Darleen started a candy business with her husband, and after
working in the business for five years—every one of which was
miserable—she admitted that opening the business was a mistake.
Once she faced the fact that the decision to operate the candy business wasn't a good one, she made another decision: to cut her
losses. She sold the candy business and started a technology training business. Running the candy business had been a painful experience, and unfortunately it took Darleen a long time to decide
to close it and start a different type of business. But she did make
a change and has never been happier.

Gene left a successful career in the construction business to go
to law school. With a wife and three children to consider, he was
not sure how he would make it work. When he was thinking about
taking the plunge, he said, "At some point I realized that the *only*
thing that stood between me and a law degree was simply the
decision to do it." When Gene described his decision-making process, he said, "I like to make decisions that have inherent guaran-
tees of success. That does not mean risk is to be avoided. To the
contrary, you can embrace risk if you focus your energy on break-
ing down any barriers to success. In the decision-making process
that I engaged in, I simply identified all the barriers and then
sought a way to overcome each barrier."

Empathy

According to Daniel Goleman, empathy builds on self-awareness.
This means that the more in tune we are with ourselves and our

emotions, the more skilled we will be in reading someone else's feelings. Your capacity or ability to know or intuit how someone else feels is key to successful interactions with others in your career discovery process. Goleman says, "The key to intuiting another's feelings is in the ability to read nonverbal channels: tone of voice, gesture, facial expression, and the like." He goes on to say that "the benefits of being able to read feelings from nonverbal cues include being better adjusted emotionally, more popular, more outgoing, and—perhaps not surprisingly—more sensitive." Your ability to understand and read other people will greatly increase your comfort level with the process of discovering work that will fulfill your needs. Being empathetic toward others will sharpen your insights about what makes people thrive and be happy in their work. You can then more easily relate these insights to your own needs and desires regarding finding new work.

There are several simple things you can do to enhance your empathy toward others:

- Ask questions and really listen to the answers.
- Respond to the answers with additional well-thought-out questions.
- Respond to body language, facial expressions, and eye contact.
- Try to understand what other people are thinking and feeling, and what may be motivating them.
- Whenever you start thinking about yourself, immediately refocus your attention on the other person.

Jonathan, who left the Fortune 50 company to search for a new career, didn't focus on his own needs. When he realized how challenging and emotionally charged a job search can be, he started investing his time in meeting and coaching other unemployed individuals. He found that by volunteering his time to offer advice and hope to others, he became more empathetic in his own career quest. As he found himself becoming more interested in other people and less focused on himself, his interactions with other people were more meaningful during his job search.

Flexibility

It can be rather difficult to pursue a new career or a new type of work without being flexible. You may prefer more structure, and as a result, you may favor following a routine that enables you to know where you will be and what you will be doing most of the time. Unfortunately, such a predictable lifestyle is difficult to achieve through the many phases of looking for gratifying work.

During this process you will be initiating conversations and having meetings with people you have never met before or don't know well. Any of these individuals may give you a new or different idea or piece of information that could be very useful to you. Being open to the unexpected is important. Saying such things as "I would never do that" will make you appear rigid to other people and could deter them from offering you helpful information.

The quest for new work usually presents constant change and ambiguity. Learning to cope with these challenges can be difficult; however, if you choose not to deal with them in a positive way or to completely resist them, you will find that your attitude will negatively affect other people's perceptions of you.

Maria, the self-employed ESL instructor and consultant, admits that she is not very flexible emotionally. Although she is constantly seeking the new, the unknown, and the next challenge, at the same time she loves the comfort of the secure and the predictable. This presents a true conflict for Maria. The way she deals with this conflict is by automatically asking herself if she is being flexible in her approach, communication, and attitude.

Humor

Humor can relieve the stress of the seemingly monumental process you are thinking of undertaking. There are so many times, situations, and circumstances during your search for gratifying work when a chuckle or a good laugh is all you need to shift your mood or change your outlook from negative to positive.

Daniel Goleman explains that happiness can actually cause physiological changes in the human brain as well as in our overall physical and psychological well-being. Happiness, he says, can bring about "an increased activity that inhibits negative feelings and fosters an increase in available energy, and a quieting of those feelings that generate worrisome thought. This configuration offers the body a general rest, as well as readiness and enthusiasm for whatever task is at hand and for striving toward a variety of goals."

A scientific explanation for this phenomenon is that laughter, which typically results from humor, stimulates endorphins in the brain, which in turn decreases physical or emotional pain. It is hoped that you won't experience too much—or any—pain during this process! At times, though, you will feel discomfort, uneasiness, or other unpleasant emotions that humor and its by-product—laughter—will relieve.

How can you generate and sustain humor?

- Keep a progressive record of your career search journey, writing down the humorous moments that occur.
- If you are experiencing stress, learn to view your experiences from an amusing perspective.
- Nurture your sense of humor by going to a comedy club, renting funny movies, and reading humorous books.
- Try to surround yourself with upbeat, smiling, happy, and lighthearted individuals. Humor is contagious!

Intelligence

Intelligence is about thinking and working smart, realizing where your intelligence lies, and taking advantage of other people's intelligence as well. While your specific career situation is very personal, remember that there are innumerable people in the world who have already experienced the same things you are going through. These people have created new work, changed careers, started and bought businesses, and accomplished everything that is discussed in this book. Intelligence is finding a handful of people who have been in the same boat and learning from their mistakes and successes.

Christina is in her late thirties and has changed careers four times already. She worked in investment banking and then became an independent event planner. After that she worked as an independent contractor, before moving into her current job running the North American operation of a global network of health managers. When asked for an example of how she demonstrated intelligence in her career changing, she said, "It is very important to develop or improve skills that you will need during the process of changing careers. At the same time, I believe that we are all good at many things and less good at other things, and we shouldn't waste our time pulling energy away from the good stuff, especially since the 'good stuff' is usually what we like best anyway."

This means that if it isn't fun or productive to reinvent the wheel while moving through the process of reshaping your work, find someone who already has and ask that person to share his or her findings with you.

Optimism

This particular quality gets a lot of attention in the world today, and deservedly so! If I had to choose three keys of the eleven that are the most basic to your success in the pursuit of satisfying work, I'd say that optimism is one of them, the other two being perseverance and curiosity. Keith Harrell, whose clients are primarily downsized workers, is the author of the book *Attitude Is Everything*. He believes that "life is not what happens to you, it's what you do about it."

Martin Seligman, PhD, the author of *Learned Optimism*, says, "Optimistic people feel that good things will last a long time and will have a beneficial effect on everything they do. They think that bad things are isolated: They won't last too long and won't affect other parts of life."

Seligman says, "Positive thinkers feel powerful, and negative thinkers feel helpless because they have been conditioned to believe that they're screwed no matter what."

Take this brief quiz to see how you score as a positive person. Circle the answer that most describes you.

1. You arrive at the airport only to find out you've missed your flight because your car service was twenty minutes late picking you up and you hit traffic on the way.
   A. You yell at the ticket agent and demand that he get you on the next flight *and* put you in first class.
   B. You politely inquire which flight is the next one to leave and then smile and say, "I had a few phone calls to make anyway."
2. You're about to give a major presentation to some senior executives at your company, and five minutes before you're scheduled to start, you can't get the LCD projector to turn on.
   A. You mutter loudly under your breath, "Goddammit, this always happens to me. When is technology ever going to work?"
   B. You announce to the group that you really think that your presentation has more impact without the Power-Point slides and plan to begin in two minutes if everyone is ready.

3. Your boss sits down with you and tells you that he's very sorry but he is going to have to let you go as part of a big organizational budget-cutting initiative.

   A. You react angrily and tell him that you'll never find another job at your same level of compensation and hope he feels good about ruining your career.

   B. You take a deep breath and say, "Well, this is a bit of a shock, so when I feel calmer, I'd like to meet with you to discuss arrangements for my separation package."

4. You have finally decided to explore a new field after taking some diagnostic tests and doing research. During your first networking meeting, the person you are talking to casually mentions that it's a tough field to break into.

   A. You go home and tell your spouse that you'll never get hired in the new industry and maybe you'd better just look for another job in your current field.

   B. You ask your networking contact what advice she would give you about the things you can do to ease your entry into the field.

5. You've been recruiting and interviewing candidates for three months for a key position in your department. You finally find the ideal candidate, and just as you're about to make her an offer, your boss tells you that he's decided not to increase the head count in your department for this fiscal year.

   A. Frustrated, you become emotional and tell your boss that he's making your job impossible to do and that you'll never hit your business goals without this new person on board.

   B. You ask your boss if you can sit down with him and have a planning meeting about ways that you can utilize other resources within your company to help you accomplish your objectives for the year. You also make an effort to stay in touch with the candidates in the hope that eventually the head count situation will turn around.

SCORE KEY

Needless to say, if you did (or really wanted to) select any "A" answers, these are not the approaches an optimist would take.

Optimism is said to be genetically predisposed; however, research has shown that environment and life experiences have just as much to do with one's tendency toward optimism. It has been proven, too, that optimism can be learned.

How can you become more optimistic?

- Whenever something negative or difficult happens, ask yourself what you've learned from your experience. Write this down so that the next time something similar happens, you're better prepared to handle it.
- If you are thinking about something in a negative way, distract yourself immediately by remembering an incident that made you laugh recently or by thinking about how you can relax over the weekend.
- It is easy to be negative if you're feeling overwhelmed. The best way to stop feeling overwhelmed is to think of everything in small steps and little pieces. What is the one thing you can do today to move toward accomplishing your goals?
- Immediately call or e-mail the most positive person you know and ask him or her to help you reframe your negative thoughts.
- Exercise. Get some fresh air. Try a new yoga class. Do something—anything—physical to change your perspective and get those endorphins flowing! The Mayo Clinic conducted a study that compared the health of more than eight hundred men and women to their scores on a personality test they had taken thirty years earlier. Those individuals

who tested high on the optimism scale years ago were 19 percent more likely to be alive than their less optimistic fellow test-takers.

- Focus on the positive aspect of your life, no matter how small: the clean bill of health you recently received from your doctor, your new haircut, the golf outing you have planned with your buddies, the big bouquet of tulips you bought for yourself, or the e-mail you just received from your old college friend.

Perseverance

Steve Mariucci, the San Francisco 49ers head coach, said, "I never wear a watch, because I always know it's now—and now is when you should do it."

Without perseverance you will not achieve at the highest levels. It is necessary for goal-setting, learning, developing and nurturing relationships, and maintaining momentum. Changing careers requires an extraordinary amount of energy and motivation, and perseverance encompasses these two things as well as focus and the desire for results. For the most part, motivation comes from inside yourself: your thoughts, your behavior, and your attitudes.

Maria received her master's degree in teaching English as a second language at the age of fifty-four. She had always gravitated toward business situations that were new and not established and believes that "drive pushes us toward uncharted territory, but eventually we decide to stop and develop what we've learned into something." In Maria's case, she designed a program for Japanese nationals on how to live and conduct business when they are sent to the United States as staff for American branches of Japanese companies. Without perseverance, Maria would not have been able to make a success of her new business. She was motivated, focused, and passionate about learning what the Japanese nationals needed and created the right program.

How can you develop perseverance? The first step is to feel passionate about your goals, about the career you have or the one you are trying to move into. Passion is very personal, and you will feel it only if what you are investigating and moving toward is right for you. If you are pursuing someone else's idea of what you should be doing, it will be nearly impossible for you to feel passionate.

Setting very specific activity goals during every phase of your search for satisfying work is a must, even for the introspective and soul-searching phase. Goals represent your purpose and the outcome you wish to achieve. Even the most motivated person will lag in his or her efforts at times without goals to work toward. Keep your goals simple, measurable, and realistic.

Find someone else who is going through a similar situation with his or her work, and agree to partner with this person in your individual searches for new work. Set up a healthy but competitive relationship to compare notes and coach each other along toward accomplishing your goals. The goals you might set for each other could include completing research on a specific industry by a specific deadline and scheduling a specific number of informational meetings. When you are held accountable in this friendly yet competitive way, you will be motivated much more than if you set goals on your own and share them with no one.

Without physical energy you will be unable to maintain a high level of motivation for long. Keep your energy level high by staying healthy, working out, and eating properly. Take time off regularly during your quest for new and satisfying work and keep your mental, emotional, and spiritual health intact. Hire a feng shui expert or an organizational consultant to help you streamline or reorganize your work environment. Think of statements or phrases that you can say to yourself to motivate you when you aren't feeling positive or focused—such as "I can do this" or "All I need to do to keep going is. . . ."

Stefanie, an independent consultant in private practice with her husband, says after having several successful careers as a psychologist, the manager of an outplacement office, and an entrepreneur, "I have huge respect for perseverance as a quality." She knows that "talent goes nowhere without perseverance. It has been a key ingredient in my career. I had the perseverance to get my PhD and to get licensed; to get promoted to run an office; to run a successful and profitable office for my employer; and to run a successful consulting practice as an entrepreneur."

Respect

My father is fond of saying, "It's just as easy to be nice." Being pleasant and gracious to everyone without exception, using good manners by always saying "Please," "Thank you," and "Excuse me," and complimenting others so they feel good about themselves are all the basics of respect. So are appreciating differences in others, being honest, listening, keeping your word, and not blaming others when something goes wrong.

You may be thinking, "Isn't this pretty obvious stuff?" Well, yes, it should be; however, we all know people who don't routinely exhibit respectful behavior to others.

Rosenbluth International, a Philadelphia-based global travel services company, actually looks for and hires candidates who are "nice." Rosenbluth has made *Fortune* magazine's 100 Best Companies to Work For in America, in part because of their effort to attract employees who share the same values, one of which is caring.

In your interactions with other people during the course of your pursuit for fulfilling work, being conscious of how considerate you are will improve your overall success.

Self-awareness

Self-awareness may well be the most complex of the eleven keys for two reasons: because of what it involves and because it's more difficult to develop. It involves knowing and understanding aspects of yourself and their relations to other people; the meaning of your appraisals and actions; your wants, intentions, and goals; and your attitudes, hopes, and fears. Without self-awareness it is nearly impossible to develop a balanced level of any of the other keys. In other words, self-awareness is at the core of balancing confidence, curiosity, decisiveness, empathy, flexibility, humor, intelligence, optimism, perseverance, and respect. On the other hand, having a high level of self-awareness does not guarantee that you will automatically command just the right amount of the other keys if you are not motivated to do so.

Self-awareness is a sophisticated form of consciousness that enables you to become the object of your own attention by being aware of your perceptions, sensations, attitudes, intentions, and emotions as well as your behaviors and general physical appearance. It is fundamentally important to possess self-awareness because it enables you to regulate yourself by self-monitoring, observing yourself, and changing your thought processes and behaviors.

The three primary sources of self-awareness are the social environment, the physical world, and one's self. The social world involves receiving verbal and nonverbal feedback from other people and deciding how relevant it is. The social environment also presents opportunities to make comparisons between yourself and others, which increases self-awareness. The physical world provides stimuli that generate self-awareness such as cameras, mirrors, recordings of your voice, newspapers, reality TV, movies, and the Internet. The third source of self-awareness is your own self, which generates self-talk, imagery, and mental and physical awareness.

Here are some exercises and activities that will help you become more self-aware.

Be Curious About Yourself

Most people tend to become either more or less curious with age. When they reach middle age, some people can become set in their ways and stop trying to understand how they come across to others. In all fairness, young people can be just as guilty of not taking risks or not trying new things. Regardless of age, curiosity is a motivational state that can emerge, change focus, or end abruptly depending on the circumstances. Much of the time, people may not try to learn more about themselves and how others view them until circumstances force them into it. Stephen is a perfect example of this. Recently, Stephen lost the job he had held for eighteen years. The day he was fired, his boss inadvertently revealed that several of Stephen's colleagues found him to be rigid and unapproachable. Stephen's wife has given him this feedback for years, but when he heard his boss say it on the day he lost his job, the comment stuck with him. When he met with his outplacement counselor, Stephen confided in her that he was embarrassed to have been viewed as inflexible by his peers. There were probably many signs that people at Stephen's company felt this way about him, but sadly, he wasn't motivated to pay attention to this feedback until it was too late to salvage the situation.

Other people become more curious and introspective as they age. They do a kind of life review assessment, and become motivated to make changes in those attitudes and behaviors that did not work well for them in the past. The key of curiosity is naturally a huge driver in this process. Reading about each of the eleven keys will help you discover your areas of strength and the areas you need to work on. Make a list of five or six people you trust and whose opinions you respect. Write down each person's name and relationship to you here:

_____

_____

_____

_____

_____

_____

_____

Next, think of several specific questions you can ask each person on your list. Ask them to answer honestly to help you learn more about yourself. Here are some examples:

- What is one thing I can do more of to enhance our relationship?
- Can you name three qualities or traits I have that you wouldn't change?
- If you could change one thing about me, what would it be and why?
- Do I have a strength that you think I could use in a different, more effective way?
- If you could give me one piece of advice to help me succeed at work, what would it be?

Receiving candid answers to these or similar questions is a great way to help you learn more about yourself and become more thoughtful about how you react and behave at work.

Write Your Own Eulogy

This exercise is typically used with people who are going through a transition of some kind and need to become more knowledgeable about themselves in order to make the transition successful. Find a quiet place to sit down and write two paragraphs that someone who knows you would read at your funeral or memorial service. Be as candid as possible and focus on the truth.

If during your search for satisfying work, you feel stymied or frustrated, review the Eleven Keys to Success. If you focus on them, you will remain grounded and secure in the knowledge that you can make the changes you need to find satisfying work!

CHAPTER 12

Job Search—the Nuts and Bolts

Your Job Search

Richard Bolles was interviewed by *Fast Company* magazine about his perspective on what has changed about finding a job since he first wrote *What Color Is Your Parachute?* The more important question, Bolles pointed out, was what had remained constant. And his answer? "Human nature. It doesn't change, and people don't like rejection; they never have and never will."

At times during your search you may feel overwhelmed, frustrated, intimidated, uncomfortable, insecure, rejected, and/or depressed. Experiencing any of these emotions is completely normal. Some people you encounter will be arrogant or insensitive or behave unprofessionally. This, too, is normal. On the positive side, there will be times when you are likely to feel euphoric, hopeful, excited, and self-confident. In fact, your job search process may amplify such positive emotions to the point where you'll wish that you could "bottle" them. Many of the people whom you will talk to or meet with will be kind, professional, complimentary, and optimistic about your chances of landing the job or work situation of your dreams. You should expect some or many of these behaviors and reactions "to come with the territory" as you continue the search for work that you love.

Now that you know where you are and where you want to be in your career, here are some tools that you can use while looking for a job. Regardless of the condition of the job market or how great an influence technology may have on the workplace, certain fundamental truths about the process of looking for a job will always remain the same.

Relationships Are Essential to Changing Jobs

The harder you work at nurturing your existing relationships, developing new ones, and revitalizing old ones, the easier and more rewarding the job search process will be for you. A relationship is not someone on a list of contacts with whom you have no real connection. A relationship involves interaction between two people in which there is consistent communication. The individuals involved are familiar with each other's work and perhaps even their life situation. Trust exists, and both people are interested in helping the other. It is a bonus when the two people in the relationship share common interests or goals and really like each other. Since relationships require a great deal of hard work, many people just aren't willing to do what is necessary to create and cultivate them. Whether or not you are conducting a job search, part of your work should always be creating new relationships and nurturing the ones you have.

What if you have let go of many of your relationships because you've buried yourself in your work? Contrary to what many people think, it is easier and makes more sense to rekindle the relationships you've let go than to try to develop new ones. The person you have had a relationship with in the past already knows you, so trust and rapport can be reignited more easily. If you haven't talked with someone in a while, it is always interesting to hear about what's changed in that person's life and work situation. She may have been wondering about you and feeling uncomfortable because she, too, hasn't done much lately to foster your relationship, and now you've done the hard part by getting in touch with her first. People inherently like to be helpful to others and are more inclined to do so with someone they already know.

New relationships are also very important in a successful job search. Ask your existing friends and acquaintances for referrals to people they know with whom you can talk. Since people tend to respond to someone they don't know if the introduction is made through someone they do, make sure to acknowledge the person whom you have in common. When beginning new relationships it is important to communicate that although you obviously are seeking their assistance, you are also approaching them to begin a mutually fulfilling relationship. This means that well after you are settled in your new job or career, you should continue to nurture these new relationships.

You Must Know Yourself

The clearer you are about your preferences, likes and dislikes, strengths and weaknesses—the essence of who you are—the more straightforward your job search process will be. By now you have gone over your self-assessments several times and have a clear sense of who you are and what you want. If you don't, go back to the chapters that describe your situation and review your self-assessments.

When you are ready to launch your job search, it is essential that you are able to tell other people, both orally and in writing, who you are, how this translates to what you are looking for, and how you can contribute and make a difference in the work you are pursuing. In the heat of a job search, people often have great difficulty articulating their interests or the ways they made improvements in previous jobs. Instead, the nervous interviewee tends to talk only about his or her present or past job tasks, responsibilities, and skills. This tendency, coupled with the likelihood that the person doing the interviewing may not be a skilled interviewer, can be a recipe for an unsuccessful job interview.

How can you prepare for interviews?

1. Think about an accomplishment you achieved in a previous job by answering these questions:

What was an obstacle, challenge, or situation that needed to be changed or improved in your job?

_____

_____

_____

_____

Fred, a human resources manager, noticed that employee turnover on the hourly levels was very high.

What did you do to change or improve it?

_____

_____

_____

_____

Fred began surveying hourly workers about their working conditions and the reasons they were dissatisfied. He then asked them for suggestions about ways to make their work more satisfactory. Using this information, Fred created a program just for hourly workers that encompassed small bonuses for meeting goals, flextime, and an allowance for technical education, and he turned an unused conference room into an employee lounge.

What was the result of the changes you made? (Use quantifiable measurements if you can, like percentages and numbers.)

_____

_____

_____

_____

Fred began tracking the hourly employee turnover rate, which went from 80 percent before he started the program to 55 percent six months after the program was in place.

2. Write down your accomplishment in one succinct sentence.

_____

_____

_____

_____

Fred can say, "I reduced hourly employee turnover from 80 percent to 55 percent by implementing a special program that motivated and rewarded hourly workers."

3. Identify three accomplishments for each job you've held, including your current position, and write them down. Practice this below:

What was an obstacle, challenge, or situation that needed to be changed or improved in your job?

_____

_____

_____

_____

What did you do to change or improve it? (Use quantifiable measurements if you can, like percentages and numbers.)

_____

_____

_____

_____

What was the result of the changes you made?

_____

_____

_____

_____

Have a Focused and Flexible Plan with Realistic, Achievable Goals

Having a written, focused, and flexible plan that includes specific action steps for achieving your goals and objectives will help ensure that you will reach your destination. A plan will also help you avoid wasting time doing things that are counterproductive.

It is ironic that when we embark on something as meaningful as looking for a job or changing careers, we rarely put a large amount of effort into planning and goal setting. Although this may be because we lack the motivation or the skills to plan, it is usually because of a psychological mind-set that accompanies our approach to the job search. Too often we become overwhelmed by the task, and yet a plan can and should be simple, specific, and flexible, with goals that are realistic, quantifiable, and small. Here is an example: Sam said he wanted a senior marketing or operations position within the consumer products industry. He wanted to secure this new career within six months and was determined to find it by actively networking with everyone he had ever met. He set the realistic goal for himself of talking with two people every week about his plan. Sam's criterion for identifying people was anyone who he felt was approachable, liked him, knew a lot of other people, or actually worked in consumer products. Using this criterion, he was able to create a long list of people. Within three months he landed a marketing executive position in New Jersey, working for an old college friend.

You should always write down your plan. Here is a sample:

My Job Search   Week of _____
These are my three primary goals:

1. Finish my résumé and show it to three people for feedback.

Did I do this?   *Yes*   *No*
Notes:

_____

_____

_____

_____

2. Make a list of fifteen people to contact with their phone numbers and e-mail addresses.

Did I do this?   *Yes*   *No*
Notes:

_____

_____

_____

_____

3. Call five people on this list with the goal of setting up a face-to-f\ace meeting with each one.

Did I do this?   *Yes*   *No*
Notes:

_____

_____

_____

_____

Save your plans each week, keeping them in one place so that you can refer to them if you need to.

You Must Make Decisions and Take Action

A plan is essential, but if you fail to make decisions or to act on the decisions you do make, your job search will be futile. Decisions drive action. Without action—making phone calls, following up those calls, setting up meetings, and scheduling interviews—it is impossible to find a new job or make the changes you'd like to make in your work. The inability to make decisions can stem from many things, including insecurity, lack of passion, and fear—fear of success, fear of failure, and fear of change or the unknown. The irony is that taking action and experiencing success is the best possible remedy for overcoming fear and vanquishing insecurity. As for not having passion, this means that either you are pursuing something you think you should do or someone else wants for you, or you simply don't have enough information. We humans just don't make decisions if we aren't motivated to do so. The first step to making decisions is learning what your motivation is.

Harold, a vice president of training, hired a career coach because he had no passion for his career and at age forty was feeling inordinately dissatisfied and unhappy. In his first meeting with his coach, Harold told her that his biggest problem, in his view, was that he was incapable of making decisions. He had changed careers twice in the past but did so easily because people he knew brought him into those jobs at a time in his life when he was younger and more flexible. Since then he had pursued careers in law, advertising, and the nonprofit sector. In each instance he had been made an offer or was set to embark on the next step when he became paralyzed about making a decision that would move him into a new career.

Harold began to make a plan every week that enabled him to make small decisions about researching industries, networking with people, answering Internet ads, and finding opportunities. He experienced a lot of highs and lows during his search, but a year and a half later he did find a job with a public relations firm. He credits his success to getting into the habit of asking himself, "What's the next decision I need to make about my job search?" until making decisions became habitual for him and no longer an obstacle.

The Most Important Elements of a Job Search

Your Résumé

The first thing that many people think about when deciding to embark on a job search is writing a résumé. Most companies still rely on résumés to learn about a candidate's work history and use it as a tool when interviewing. Another reason for knowing who you are, what you want, and what you have to offer is that you can put this information on your résumé. Although a résumé serves as documentation of your career history, it has three even more important purposes:

1. Writing a good résumé requires you to spend quality time thinking about who you are and the impact you've made in the past. Once you have done this, it will be much easier for you to handle face-to-face discussions with a networking contact or interviewer.

2. You can creatively describe your experiences and accomplishments in a way that can effectively match the interviewer's needs.

3. The opportunity to express your unique personality traits and skills on paper can help you distinguish yourself from other candidates.

Writing a résumé for the Internet is a different process from writing your résumé for a human being to hold in his or her hand. There are hundreds of thousands of jobs listed on the Internet, and you'll need to create an online-compatible résumé with keywords in a different text form in order to post it. While the Internet is a powerful and ubiquitous tool for you to use in your job search, ultimately a human being will be sitting in a room with you, reading your résumé. So creating two versions is a good idea. Here are some differences between an online résumé and a traditional résumé:

ONLINE RÉSUMÉ	TRADITIONAL RÉSUMÉ
Noun-heavy with a focus on keywords. For example, keywords might be *Java*, *nonprofit*, *purchasing*, *consumer products*, and *human resources*. These keywords are usually placed at the beginning or the end of your résumé rather than the middle.	Verb-heavy with a focus on action. Examples of action verbs are *succeeded*, *originated*, *devised*, *created*, and *managed*.
Focus is on describing a specific job in your career history, one that is closest to the job you are applying for.	Organized from a chronological standpoint, listing all the jobs you've had in your career.
Should be as simple and plain as possible without unusual fonts or graphic elements.	Can be more creatively designed with different typefaces and spacing.
Can be any length, but typos are even more glaring when picked up by a scanner.	No longer than two pages, and typos aren't acceptable on this version either.

Your résumé represents you and is often what people use to assess you even before you meet. Because of this you should write the best résumé possible. On the other hand, spending more time writing your résumé than planning your job search strategy will not be the best use of your time.

Networking

Networking will always be an important part of the job search process, so you should become comfortable with it. Learning to network is analogous to learning how to ride a bicycle. When you were little, it seemed so impossible to learn to ride a two-wheeler. But once you learned how, it was exhilarating at first and then became second nature. Now you can't imagine not being able to remember how to ride a bike. If you've gone a while without riding one, you will feel a bit wobbly at first, but then you will hit your familiar stride.

Fear of the unknown is perfectly normal. Being fearful of unpleasant experiences is normal, too. If you are fearful of networking, the best way to handle your anxiety is to think of the worst possible scenario. Ask yourself, "What's the worst that could happen?" Chances are your fear will be harder to deal with than the actual negative or unpleasant outcome that might result from your taking a risk. If you are fearful of being rejected, remind yourself that it is unlikely people will reject you as a person in a networking situation. They may not take the time to talk with or meet you because they either don't know how to help you or don't see the value in it. Since there are so many people who do engage in networking, it makes sense just to move on if you are getting either a negative response or no response from a particular individual.

Here are some ways to begin the networking process:

1. Make a list of everyone you know and divide them into categories such as professional services, neighbors, former business colleagues, friends, and college alumni. You will be continually surprised by the people who will help you during your networking process, like your dentist or neighbor three doors down.

2. It is ideal if you purchase contact management software such as Act! or Outlook to keep your network organized. Whether or not you do this, be sure to keep all the names and contact information in one place.

3. Before you e-mail or call anyone on your list, write a brief script stating what it is you're looking for. Be specific and succinct. Your script will have an introduction, something like "I can't believe it's been two years since we've talked. How are you doing?" Then describe what you're doing in one or two sen-

tences: "I'm calling you because I've decided to make a career change, and I had heard that you did the same thing about a year ago." The last part of the script discusses a next step: "I'd be so appreciative if we could spend twenty minutes together so that you can share your experience with me. When would this be convenient for you?"

4. Go to the networking meeting prepared with a résumé (if appropriate) and a business card. (Even if you are unemployed, have simple business cards printed with your name and contact information.) You should also know what two or three pieces of information you are looking for. Are you looking for feedback on your résumé or the names of people at a specific company? If you don't do this, the information you gather may not be useful to you.

5. Always ask the person if there is anything you can do to help him or her. The person could be looking for a new babysitter or is trying to buy a new car, and you may be able to offer help as well.

6. Your networking style is crucial. The impression you make really matters. Be sure that you look and sound professional and confident. Don't ramble on and on about yourself.

7. Any gathering of people presents an opportunity for you to network. Baseball games, association meetings, your neighborhood block party, and the grocery store are all full of people who know what's going on in the business world and know other people.

8. Always send a thank-you note or e-mail to the person immediately after your meeting. Say that you plan to stay in touch periodically. You should initiate follow-up, particularly if the person has offered to send you someone's name or other information.

9. Online social networking is a significant element of networking; however, it will never replace traditional face-to-face networking. It is a good idea to update your profile regularly on the social networking Web sites of your choice, such as LinkedIn

and Plaxo, as well as to reach out to your online connections, posting and answering questions and writing and requesting recommendations. A word of caution: The majority of employers and headhunters will google you or go directly to your online networking profiles. If you or your friends have posted inappropriate photos or comments on your Facebook or MySpace profiles, this can mar your professional reputation and possibly damage your chances of getting an interview.

Networking is a life skill, not just something you do when you are changing jobs. The more you practice it, the more useful it will become to you, not only during your time of transition but even when you are happily working.

Answering Job Board or Newspaper Ads

While both newspaper and job board ads are very useful job search tools, they are no longer the primary way to get a job and haven't been for quite a while. Companies today are becoming much more creative in their approaches to recruiting new employees—placing ads on buses and subways and on craigslist.org, for example. Many offer financially rewarding referral programs for existing employees with links on their company Web sites that list descriptions of current job openings. By all means answer ads if you'd like, keeping in mind that this conventional method is not the most warm, interactive, or multidimensional way to communicate with a potential employer.

Contingency and Search Firms

Contingency firms are used by companies to find candidates in a specific salary range—usually under $100,000. They don't normally sign a contract with the company for whom they are recruiting candidates and are paid a fee only when a candidate is hired. Search (or retainer) firms are used by companies for filling senior-level positions, typically those that pay $100,000 or more. Search firms sign an agreement and receive their fee in installments even if they never find a candidate who is hired by the company.

Both types of firms have one client: the company that hires them. Most of the time if you are a job candidate who has been contacted by a search or contingency firm, you will feel as if the recruiter or search professional does not have your best interests at heart. It will seem as if they pay attention to you only when they think you might be fit for a specific opening. And you will be absolutely right! The sooner you realize and accept this fact, the less frustrated you will be when dealing with contingency and search firms.

Go ahead and work with search or contingency firms, but do not rely solely on them to find your next job for you. In most cases they will only be able to place you if you are looking for exactly the same type of position in the industry you work in now. *Rarely is a search firm paid a fee for placing a candidate who is making a career change.* Still, it's smart to develop long-standing relationships with search or contingency professionals even if they can't place you. Refer candidates to them and always return their calls when they leave a message asking whom you might know for a search they are working on. A search or contingency professional is a good person to develop a networking relationship with over time. Just remember that they are salespeople whose compensation is contingent upon placing individuals with specific skills in specific jobs.

Interviewing

It is highly unusual to find a new job without going on a face-to-face interview, and these days, it is also common to meet and talk to a large number of people in an organization during the hiring process. If you are not capable of making an impressive presentation to the people with whom you are interviewing, you will not receive a job offer.

"Performing" well in interviews means several things: Your physical image must be appealing to the interviewer; your verbal presentation must be interesting and focused on what you can bring to and do for the interviewer and his or her company;

and you must demonstrate that you will fit well in the organization.

Interviewing, while stressful for many people, is a learned skill. Being prepared to talk about yourself and your past accomplishments succinctly and in a compelling manner is very important. If you've gone through some assessment and written a quality résumé, then you already are familiar with all this information. Since you probably don't go on interviews every day, it is difficult to practice, but before going on a significant interview, ask friends, family, or a career coach to role-play with you. Oddly enough, most people don't do this. Preparing a list of questions for the interviewer and asking the same ones of everyone you meet at the company is another good idea. You can write down their answers, compare them later, and use the information to write customized thank-you notes. Here are some questions you might want to ask:

- What do you think an average day in this position would be like?
- What would be your expectations of me in my first three months? Six months? A year?
- What are the biggest problems or challenges you are facing in this department or division?
- What reporting relationships would I have in this job?
- What kinds of people succeed here?
- What were the strengths of the person who was in this job previously?
- How would you describe the corporate culture here?

Remember that many people aren't necessarily very skilled at interviewing candidates. It is therefore your responsibility as the interviewee to keep the conversation on track so that (1) you can communicate everything you need to the interviewer before the interview ends, and (2) you will get the information you need in order to move forward in the process.

Branding

A relatively new aspect of the job search is the concept of branding yourself. While large companies have had marketing departments who have done this for years, it is now recommended that those of you who are reinventing yourselves or simply looking for another job similar to one you've had should do the same thing.

In a 2009 article on www.lifehack.org, it is recommended that you focus on five things before creating your own personal brand:

1. Brainstorm a mission and vision statement. Your mission is what you do every day and includes your values and traits. Your vision describes what you want to do in the future.
2. Create your personal brand statement. This positions you in the minds of others and tells people what you do and who you serve.
3. Give yourself a slogan. Very few individuals have their own slogan, yet many companies rely on them to connect people to their brand. Catchy and original are the keys here.
4. Figure out your brand attributes. In an interview when you are asked to describe yourself, this is how you would respond.
5. Find your audience. Your audience isn't just people who will hire you but also those who pay attention to your work and spread the word to others.

Implementing your brand can be accomplished in many ways, including the following:

1. Write a blog.
2. Respond to others' blog entries.
3. Write articles in professional and trade publications.
4. Post and answer questions on LinkedIn.

5. Create your own personal Web site. Even if you don't design it right now, go to GoDaddy.com or Homestead.com and purchase and register a domain name.
6. Conduct polls on Facebook or other social networking sites.
7. Present at professional conferences or to nonprofit groups.
8. Tweet your followers on Twitter about your whereabouts and actions.

Follow-up

Writing thank-you notes is a very important method of follow-up for both networking meetings and actual interviews. Whether your thanks are word-processed, handwritten, or in an e-mail isn't really the issue. Just do it! It adds to the positive impression the interviewer has of you. It also is an additional opportunity to sell yourself and to address any concerns on the interviewer's part that may have come up during the interview. Joanne, the vice president of human resources at an international trading company, observed that, sadly, only 10 percent of the applicants she interviews for nonexempt jobs and 50 percent of the applicants she interviews for exempt or managerial positions send thank-you notes. Marj, a director of human resources at a large utility, stated, "I think thank-you letters are becoming rarer and rarer, regardless of the job levels." This is too bad since, as she explains, these notes are another tool an applicant has. "They are a good way for a candidate to remind the interviewer of his or her name, reiterate interest in the position, and do a little sales pitch, too."

Everyone has had some experience looking for a job. Regardless of what this has been, there are several false beliefs about looking for a job that perpetually circulate and people seem to accept. This next section addresses the most prevalent myths and the truth about them.

Job Search Myths

Myths that people believe about looking for a job are many and persistent. The most common ones are these:

Myth #1: A résumé should be only one page.

Absolutely not! The normal length of a résumé is two to three pages (at most). It is fine to have addendum pages such as a list of references or published articles. A one-page résumé is only appropriate for a recent college grad.

Myth #2: If you go on an interview through a contingency or search firm, you cannot speak directly to the person who interviewed you after the interview.

The person who interviewed you is either a decision-maker or an influencer in the hiring process. Ask him during the interview if he minds if you contact him with any questions you may have later. If he says no, be skeptical about his interest or style. After all, you are the person who was on the interview, not the recruiting professional who set up your interview. He or she is also someone you can nurture as a networking contact even if you aren't hired.

Myth #3: If eight people at a company interviewed you, you need to send a thank-you note only to the person you'd report to if you got the job.

Those other seven people took their valuable time to interview you. Of course you should send each one a thank-you note!

Myth #4: You shouldn't take notes during an interview.

Why not? Nobody has a photographic memory while talking, listening, and processing information. Simply ask the interviewer politely if she minds if you take some notes. Obviously, you should use abbreviations or keywords so that you're not concentrating too hard on taking notes and not focusing enough on the conversation.

Myth #5: There is no point in conducting a job search during the summer or in December because companies aren't hiring then.

This is absolutely ridiculous. In fact, during the summer, businesspeople are more casual and "laid back" in their attitudes and approaches. They don't tend to be as immersed in stressful projects. What a great time to approach people! In December, companies may be focused on bringing someone on board before the new calendar or fiscal year. People are in a much more celebratory mood during this time of year, and December offers lots of opportunities for networking.

Myth #6: The most qualified candidate has the best shot at getting a job offer.

Obviously, for most positions, a company needs someone with specific skills and experience. It is also true that many companies still lean toward someone who has worked in the same industry. It is more likely that the individual who *fits* into the company culture is the one who will get the offer. This means that as a candidate you are accountable for finding out and understanding what the culture is—the values that shape the company, the way people communicate, and the kinds of people who are respected within the organization. You will not find this kind of information on a Web site or in an annual report. You will find it from talking to people—the company's employees, vendors, and ex-employees.

Myth #7: Only certain components of a job offer are negotiable.

The two best times to negotiate with a company are when they ask you to join them, and when they ask you to leave. Anything can be negotiated if you are very clear about what you need and want, and can state the reasons why. You stand the best chance of getting your needs met if you put yourself in the company's shoes during the negotiation. Not only can compensation be negotiated but also the work itself, the way you will do the work, whom you will report to, and every other aspect of the job.

Looking for a new job requires many skills, and the more you network, interview, and negotiate, the easier the process becomes. Above all, trust your instincts during your job search. As with any relationship, you may have to make compromises. However, there is absolutely no reason that you shouldn't be able to find the right job—a job that fits your personality and fulfills your needs.

Afterword

Gallup Poll's survey in late 2008 showed that worker satisfaction is down from previous years, particularly in the areas of the recognition they receive at work (only 45 percent are completely satisfied), the amount of work that is required (50 percent are completely satisfied), the amount of on-the-job stress (27 percent are completely satisfied), and chances for promotion (35 percent are completely satisfied).

These statistics point to a pervasive dissatisfaction in the workplace today. On the other hand, it is now both accepted and expected that if you are unhappy, bored, or unfulfilled in your work, you *can* and *should* change what you are doing. In Salary.com's 2008/2009 annual job satisfaction survey, nearly 80 percent of employers do not believe that employees will begin a job search, in part because of the down economy. By contrast, 60 percent of the employees surveyed intend to intensify their job search in the next three months despite the economy. The top reasons they would like new jobs? Inadequate compensation, inadequate development, and insufficient recognition.

Work is no longer just about completing tasks to make money for a company and its shareholders. Instead, it is about creating and maintaining a more equitable relationship between employee and employer or business owner and client. It is also about you as an individual needing and wanting choices, meaning, rewards, motivation, and success in your work. The path is different for each of us. If you are feeling dissatisfied or disillusioned with your current job, then your mission is not only to admit that you are dissatisfied, but to commit to creating a vision for the kind of work that will bring you satisfaction and to design a plan for implementing your vision. You can begin the journey of finding gratifying work right now!

There are thousands upon thousands of people who have successfully changed their work to reflect their needs and preferences. Here are a few stories of people who have done so and are happy.

Rita is a self-employed media consultant. At forty-six she has taken what she's learned in the six careers she's already had (recruiting, the restaurant business, social services counseling, real estate sales, corporate relocation, and advertising sales) and created interesting new work for herself. "I've always wanted to do work that matters to me. I need to be passionate about what I do, and I want to excel at it. Recently, I stepped off the cliff of the more secure corporate environment and have been successful in establishing myself as an independent consultant—*and* I have enough work to be financially secure."

Greg, fifty-two, was a lawyer for twenty years. "I had to give in to the creative parts of me that I had not been pursuing during that career," he says. So he decided to stop practicing law and become a photographer. He now reports: "My job gives me the opportunity to make things with my hands, which is a kind of creativity that is most important to me."

At thirty-six, Jon was downsized from his job as a corporate human resources executive. He intentionally took more than a year off from working to "figure out what I wanted to do." Why? While he was successful in his job, he did not find it fulfilling. "I thought I was sophisticated when I started my introspective journey and found it more difficult than I had expected. There's no language and no definite path to searching for the right work. I do feel that there is a path that is different for everyone." While Jon knows he needs to find challenging and engaging work, at the same time he wants to live a more holistic life, something he believes is difficult to do while one is caught up in the corporate whirlwind.

During his hiatus, Jon went through an extensive rediscovery process using the Crystal-Barkley method (*The Crystal-Barkley Guide to Taking Charge of Your Career* by Nella Barkley and Eric Sandburg), which included writing a thirty-page story of his life. What did he decide to do? He thinks he'll end up in human resources again, but with an employer who believes strongly in human capital and isn't simply focused on making a profit. Now that he has refreshed his understanding of himself and what is important to him, Jon feels better equipped to find fulfillment—as opposed to just "success"—in his work.

While it is important to experience tangible success in your work—that is, achieving the business goals that you and your employer have set—once you have done this, the meaning can fade quickly. Teri, thirty-five, sells a music service. She has ranked as the number-one salesperson in her company for six years. Teri is Bored and Plateaued. "Who cares if I make the top of the list again?" she says. "It just does not mean anything to me anymore." Teri is planning a start-up venture, manufacturing and selling acrylic frames for parents' ultrasound pictures of their babies in utero. "This is a project from my heart, so I love it," says Teri. "Ultraframes fuel my creative side. This will be a huge challenge—I cannot wait."

Miguel practiced law his entire career. At sixty he bought a wine store franchise, opening a brand-new location for the franchisor. In his first six months Miguel's sales ranked in the top percentage of all the company's franchises in the United States. More important, Miguel is "extremely satisfied and gratified to be working for myself and deciding on my own destiny and future." Miguel had been in the Yearning to Be on Your Own situation for a long time because "I was tired and fed up working for incompetent managers who were where they were because of who they knew and not what they knew. I just wanted to be the 'captain of my own ship.'"

Jack retired at sixty-three from a thirty-year career in the chemical industry. At sixty-nine he works full-time as a senior consultant for a research company that supports his former industry. He holds three significant leadership roles for volunteer organizations as well. When Jack isn't working sixty hours a week, he flies a plane, sails, kayaks, and collects cameras. When Jack was asked how long he thought he'd keep working, he replied, "Probably another ten years."

In her book *What Do You Want to Do When You Grow Up?* psychologist Dorothy Cantor makes an important point that "previously defined visions can fade in importance over time. Life keeps happening, and transitions are part of it." The point of this book is to help you realize that being satisfied, happy, fulfilled, or exhilarated with your work is up to you and you alone.

Caroline, at forty, owns a contracting/consulting company. She works with engineering firms as a program manager for a technical research project on rail transportation crashworthiness and safety. Both her bachelor's and master's degrees are in engineering, but when she actually worked as an engineer, she was never truly satisfied. Now she uses her engineering background in a nonengineering role and finds her work very meaningful. With two children, Caroline needs to work to supplement her husband's income, yet she is able to have some downtime between consulting projects.

Caroline created her own work by taking self-assessment tests, which helped her define her strengths and interests. Then she took action by designing work that would enable her to bring in income and spend time with her young children.

When Caroline responded to the question "Are you satisfied with your current job?" this was her answer: "I absolutely LOVE what I do. I enjoy managing and scheduling my own time; I enjoy the extreme diversity of my jobs. I like being able to do something else during the downtimes of one contract and having an impact on two separate projects, instead of whittling my time away on one job and filling in the downtimes with unnecessary busywork."

It is time to make yourself happy in your work. Start your journey today. As Jon, the human resources executive, said earlier, it's not necessarily easy to find your path toward finding satisfying work. This is why more people choose *not* to do anything about alleviating their unhappiness or dissatisfaction. Don't let yourself be one of them. Instead, close your eyes and allow yourself to imagine what it would feel like to be happy and excited and fulfilled in your work. Finding work that is satisfying, gratifying, and fulfilling will change your life!

Resources

Chapter 1: Why Do You Want or Need to Change Your Work?

Bridging the Generation Gap: How to Get Radio Babies, Boomers, Gen-Xers, and Gen-Yers to Work Together and Achieve More by Linda Gravett and Robin Throckmorton. Career Press, 2007. A guide for anyone who works with other generations and needs to learn to understand the point of view of each generation. The authors write in two distinct voices—as a baby boomer and as a Gen Xer—and identify the differences and similarities across generations.

Life's a Bitch and Then You Change Careers: 9 Steps to Get Out of Your Funk and On to Your Future by Andrea Kay. STC Paperbacks, 2006. Career consultant Kay lays out her time-tested, nine-step program to show people how to make a shift out of a career they hate.

Chapter 2: What Is Your Work Situation?

Escape from Corporate America: A Practical Guide to Creating the Career of Your Dreams by Pamela Skillings. Ballantine Books, 2008. This humorous and insightful book shares dozens of stories of people who have escaped from their cubicles. More important, Skillings provides questionnaires and assessments to help readers figure out their dream job and plot and "escape" from corporate America.

You Majored in What? Mapping Your Path from Chaos to Career by Katharine Brooks. Viking, 2009. Published during times of high unemployment, this book helps recent college grads figure out and find a career that fits, regardless of their major.

Get the Job You Want, Even When No One's Hiring by Ford R. Myers. Wiley, 2009. This book offers timely and relevant advice for those job seekers who have been laid off or are eager to find work that makes them happy despite the tough economic times.

One Person/Multiple Careers: A New Model for Work/Life Success by Marci Alboher. Warner Business Books, 2007. This book offers dozens of stories of real people who have created a living by meshing a variety of skills and experiences.

An Interesting Web Site

Fast Company magazine. *www.fastcompany.com.* A site that is designed to guide you through various career cycles, including building your business, leading your team, going solo, reinventing yourself, launching your career, and being a change agent. It provides customized stories, interactive tools, and expert opinions, all focused on your career in the "new economy."

Chapter 3: Values, Attitudes, and Change Resilience, and Chapter 4: Personality Preferences, Interests, and Favorite Skills

StrengthsFinder 2.0: A New and Upgraded Edition of the Online Test from Gallup's Now, Discover Your Strengths by Tom Rath. Gallup Press, 2007. An updated version of Gallup's online assessment, StrengthsFinder, this book helps the reader identify his strengths and create an action-planning guide for applying these strengths.

Do What You Are: Discover the Perfect Career for You Through the Secrets of Personality Type by Paul Tieger and Barbara Barron-

Tieger. Little, Brown, 2007, 4th ed. Based on the Myers Briggs Type Indicator, this book introduces personality types and aligns them with suggested careers. Many occupations are listed that are popular with specific personality types, including careers in biotech, new media, e-commerce, and telecommunications.

Career Match: Connecting Who You Are with What You'll Love to Do by Shoya Zichy with Ann Bidou. AMACOM, 2007. This entertaining and witty book uses a workstyle assessment technique called Color Q, which is basically a twist on personality type.

Some Useful Web Sites

CareerPerfect.com. *www.careerperfect.com.* A comprehensive career-planning site with online career-planning tools and tests; advice for and samples of résumés, e-résumés, and cover letters; job search advice and resources; interview advice and tools; and articles on such topics as employment trends and coping with unemployment.

CareerPlanner.com. *www.careerplanner.com.* This site provides information on the career-planning process, a reading list in career planning, and some career-planning tests, some which cost a fee to take.

Careers by Design. *www.careers-by-design.com.* This site offers affordable, statistically reliable, and valid assessments for individual career planning, determining personality type, and corporate team development (Strong Interest Inventory, MBTI, FIRO-B, 16PF).

ERICAE.NET. *www.ericae.net.* A clearinghouse for assessment, evaluation, and research information.

JobBankUSA.com. *www.jobbankusa.com.* In addition to being a job search clearinghouse, the site offers a free career analysis, including the Motivational Appraisal of Personal Potential (MAPP), to discover natural motivations, interests, and talents for work.

Chapter 5: Where's the Meaning?

Career Renegade: How to Make a Great Living Doing What You Love by Jonathan Fields. Broadway Books, 2009. Written primarily for employees who are dissatisfied with their jobs. There are sections on how to determine the exact work path to choose, with inspiring interviews of successful career changers.

Change Your Career: Transitioning to the Nonprofit Sector by Laura Gassner Otting. Kaplan, 2007. So many people who have had for-profit careers are drawn toward a new career involving making a difference for a cause close to their heart. Otting shares her wisdom and passion for anyone finding themselves in this position and makes it feel like a real possibility.

Volunteer Vacations: Short-Term Adventures That Will Benefit You and Others by Bill McMillon, Doug Cutchins, Anne Geissinger, and Ed Asner. Chicago Review Press, 2009. This is a comprehensive guidebook for people who want to travel and find fulfilling and stimulating temporary work.

Green Careers: Choosing Work for a Sustainable Future by Jim Cassio and Alice Rush. New Society Publishers, 2009. This book is ideal for students, career changers, and job seekers who are passionate about the greening of the world. Details of ninety different professions in twelve career groups are described.

The Artist's Way by Julia Cameron. Jeremy P. Tarcher/Putnam, 1992. This classic unfolds a twelve-week program for recovering creativity using journaling as a method for doing so. It was written for artists and people in creative occupations, but it is a useful guide for nonartists as well.

The Nonprofit Career Guide: How to Land a Job That Makes a Difference by Shelly Cryer. Fieldstone Alliance, 2008. This book unfolds a comprehensive and very clear road map for anyone who is considering a career in the not-for-profit sector. It includes information about key trends, as well as an overview of the various job opportunities that are available in the nonprofit arena and is useful for both job seekers and career coaches.

Test-Drive Your Dream Job: A Step-by-Step Guide to Finding and Creating the Work You Love by Brian Kurth. Business Plus, 2008. This hands-on program from the founder of VocationVacations offers lists of questions, charts, and reality checks about money, health insurance, and the impact of a life change.

How'd You Score That Gig? by Alexandra Levit. Ballantine Books, 2008. Levit describes eight types of people, including the Creator, the Data Head, the Networker, and the Nurturer. She then identifies eight jobs within each category.

Some Nonprofit Organizations

American Red Cross. *www.redcross.org.* This organization helps keep people safe every day as well as in emergencies. 800-662-2531.

America's Promise—The Alliance for Youth, led by Colin Powell. *www.americaspromise.org.* The organization's focus is on improving the lives of America's youth through mentoring and other support efforts. 703-684-4500.

FeedingAmerica.org. *www.feedingamerica.org.* This is the nation's largest domestic hunger relief organization. 800-771-2303.

Global Volunteers. *www.globalvolunteers.org.* This is a private, international tax-exempt organization in special consultative status with the United Nations. 800-487-1074.

Habitat for Humanity. *www.habitat.org.* This organization works in partnership with people in need of building and renovating decent, affordable housing. 800-442-5914.

Literacy Volunteers of America. *www.literacyvolunteers.org.* This organization recruits and trains volunteers who teach English to people who speak other languages. 877-435-7582.

Some Useful Web Sites

www.nationalservice.gov. This government-sponsored site promotes volunteering in America and offers tools and information about national and community service to people who want to make a difference through community service and volunteering.

VocationVacations. *www.vocationvacations.com.* This innovative Web site provides more than 125 unique "vacations" where you can work alongside a professional in your dream career. Mentors in jobs such as radio talk host, winemaker, TV scriptwriters, and interior designers show you the ropes in their work environments.

Bridgespan.org. *www.bridgespan.org.* This Web site helps nonprofits and philanthropies reach their goals and features careers in nonprofit organizations.

Chapter 6: Been There, Done That, but Still Need to Earn

Busting Loose from the Business Game: Mind-Blowing Strategies for Recreating Yourself, Your Team, Your Business, and Everything in Between by Robert Scheinfeld. Wiley, 2009. This book helps you discover who you really are, what you're capable of, and how you can transform your experience of business—particularly in the areas of sales, marketing, profits, cash flow, and taxes.

The Secret of Shelter Island: Money and What Matters by Alexander Green. Wiley, 2009. Financial analyst Alexander Green explores the complicated relationship we all have with money and reveals his road map to a rich life despite tough economic times.

Suze Orman's 2009 Action Plan by Suze Orman. Spiegel & Grau, 2009. Orman, the nation's go-to expert on financial matters, describes what needs to be done to take action on your financial goals rather then waiting out the economic downturn.

Chapter 7: Bruised and Gun-shy

Thank You for Firing Me! How to Catch the Next Wave of Success After You Lose Your Job by Candice Reed and Kitty Martini. Sterling, 2010. This book was written by two authors who've been fired—and it was the best thing that ever happened to them. This humorous, reassuring resource book is a compass for navigating the new economy for those who are jobless. Now is the time to size up new career opportunities, bounce back, and rebuild.

Why Work Sucks and How to Fix It: No Schedules, No Meetings, No Joke—the Simple Change That Can Make Your Job Terrific by Cali Ressler and Jody Thompson. Portfolio, 2008. The theme of this book is to change your focus from hours to outcomes in order to become more productive, happier, and less stressed.

Carve Your Own Road: Do What You Love and Live the Life You Envision by Jennifer Remling and Joe Remling. Career Press, 2009. This book offers a process for reconnecting with your dreams and expanding your opportunities in your work.

A Useful Web Site

www.jobstresshelp.com. This site provides tips and statistics on how to deal with the stress that work can create. Responses to various surveys conducted on workplace stress are shown.

Chapter 8: Bored and Plateaued

Beyond Boredom and Anxiety: Experiencing Flow in Work and Play by Mihaly Csikszentmihalyi. Jossey-Bass, 2000; special 25th anniversary edition. This revolutionary book is viewed as one of the premier books about what motivates behavior.

The Pathfinder by Nicholas Lore. Simon & Schuster, 1998. This comprehensive book is still one of the best-rated guides for moving you through the process of designing the career you want. It is filled with self-tests and diagnostic tools to help you understand yourself and design work that will fit your personality, goals, needs, and values.

Chapter 9: Yearning to Be on Your Own

Being a Consultant or Independent Contractor

Getting Started in Consulting by Alan Weiss. Wiley, 2009, 3rd ed. Weiss is the guru of consulting, and this edition of his best-selling book is more comprehensive than ever and up-to-date with Weiss's usual practical guidance.

How to Make It Big as a Consultant by William A. Cohen. AMA-COM, 2009, 4th ed. This focused book is filled with advice for starting up and maintaining a lucrative consulting practice. This edition is a must to keep an arm's length away.

Consulting for Dummies by Nelson and Peter Economy. For Dummies, 2008, 2nd ed. Crammed with practical and proven tips and techniques, this newly revised edition is great for established and novice consultants.

Some Useful Web Sites

Guru.com. *www.guru.com.* This site acts as a clearinghouse for consultants and employers. Projects are posted ranging from Web site design and legal work to writing and graphic design.

Institute of Management Consultants. *www.imcusa.org.* This is the site for the preeminent professional association for management and business consultants.

Buying a Franchise

The Educated Franchisee: The How-to Book for Choosing a Winning Franchise by Rick Bisio with Mike Kohler. Bascom Hill Publishing Group, 2008. As one of the most respected franchise consultants in the United States, Bisio shares his secrets for success in owning franchised businesses.

The Franchise Fraud: How to Protect Yourself Before and After You Invest by Robert L. Purvin Jr. BookSurge Publishing, 2008. This book exposes the risks and fraud that many companies perpetuate on their franchisees. It outlines what to ask, what agreements to make, and how to take advantage of the worthwhile franchising opportunities that are available.

A Useful Web Site

www.franchise.com. This site provides information on buying domestic and international franchises, finding real estate, and financing your franchise.

Buying a Business

The Complete Guide to Buying a Business by Fred Steingold. NOLO, 2007, 2nd ed. This book shows you how to do everything you need to do to purchase a business. It explains how to find the right business, analyze the seller's numbers, negotiate a payment plan, and work with lawyers, accountants, and brokers.

How to Buy and/or Sell a Small Business for Maximum Profit: A Step-by-Step Guide by Rene V. Richards. Atlantic Publishing, 2006. This book is geared toward the novice entrepreneur who wants to buy or sell a small business. Topics are comprehensive and include raising capital, using discounted cash flow, and understanding buyouts, letters of intent, legal and tax concerns, and contracts.

A Useful Web Site

www.bizbuysell.com. This site lists thousands of established businesses for sale, forms, checklists, and interactive worksheets, plus recommendations of articles, books, and Web sites to help you buy a business.

Marketing and Selling How-tos

Startup Guide to Guerrilla Marketing: A Simple Battle Plan for First-Time Marketers by Jay Conrad Levinson. Entrepreneur Press, 2007. Levinson is the father of guerrilla marketing and author of fifty-five other business books. His strategies for start-up businesses on tight budgets have been embraced by millions.

The New Rules of Marketing and PR: How to Use News Releases, Blogs, Podcasting, Viral Marketing, and Online Media to Reach Buyers Directly by David Meerman Scott. Wiley, 2007. A great guide for the technical novice on the basics of digital marketing and ways to harness the Internet to lead customers into the buying process.

Starting Your Own Business

No Limits: How I Escaped the Clutches of Corporate America to Live the Self-employed Life of My Dreams by Sara Morgan. Custom Solutions LLC, 2009. If you feel unsatisfied with your current work situation or have a great idea for self-employment, but lack the courage to move forward, this book is for you.

Entrepreneur's Notebook: Practical Advice for Starting a New Business Venture by Steven K. Gold. Learning Ventures Press, 2006. A serial entrepreneur, Gold has written an invaluable reference for entrepreneurs in the start-up phase.

The Knack: How Street-Smart Entrepreneurs Learn to Handle Whatever Comes Up by Norm Brodsky and Bo Burlingham. Portfolio, 2008. Writers for *Inc.* magazine, Brodsky and Burlingham bring readers into the nitty-gritty practicalities of running your own business, such as raising capital, customer relationships, and hiring good management talent.

On Competition by Michael Porter. Harvard Business School Press, 2008. Porter distinguishes between operational effectiveness and competitive strategy, a concept many entrepreneurs struggle with. Porter has a unique ability to bridge theory and practice.

The Small Biz Balancing Act: Secrets to Restoring Passion and Play in Business and Life by Victoria Munro. Top Flight Press LLC, 2009. Author Munro shares the secrets she's learned from launching and running nine different businesses.

Small Business Start-Up Kit by Peri Pakroo. NOLO, 2008. This user-friendly guide about how to launch a business is loaded with tips, tear-out forms, and instructions.

Writing a Business Plan

Writing a Convincing Business Plan by Arthur deThomas and Stephanie Derammelaere. Barron's Educational Series, 2008, 3rd ed. This book shows how to organize and write a logical, business-savvy, and professional business plan that can be presented to banks and potential investors.

The New Business Road Test: What Entrepreneurs and Executives Should Do Before Writing a Business Plan by John Mullins. Financial Times Press, 2008, 2nd ed. This book provides a reality check before even writing a business plan.

Some Useful Web Sites

Bplans.com. *www.bplans.com.* In addition to advice on topics ranging from starting a business to helpful business software to reading lists for effective start-ups, this site includes a variety of sample business plans you can search that match your business.

Inc. magazine. *www.Inc.com.* This site contains information about how to plan and start a small business and advice for small business owners about such topics as technology, hiring and motivating employees, marketing, and customer service.

Success magazine. *www.Successmagazine.com.* This site contains trends, tips, and ideas for entrepreneurs as well as profiles of successful entrepreneurs.

U.S. Small Business Administration. *www.sba.gov.* A vast site with information on starting a business, financing, business opportunities, disaster assistance, local offices, SCORE resources in your area, and more.

MyLLCAgreement.com. *www.myllcagreement.com.* A site that offers free to low-cost LLC agreements along with phone or online support for any entrepreneur or business owner.

LegalZoom.com. *www.legalzoom.com.* A site that offers low-cost legal document services such as incorporations, LLCs, trademarks, patents, and copyrights.

Entrepreneur magazine. *www.entrepreneur.com.* This site is rich with resources for new business ideas, writing a marketing plan, raising financing, and growing your business.

Chapter 10: One Toe in the Retirement Pool

The Joy of Retirement: Finding Happiness, Freedom, and the Life You've Always Wanted by David C. Borchard and Patricia A. Donohoe. AMACOM, 2008, Kindle ed. Author Borchard shows baby boomers in their fifties and sixties how to reinvent themselves through planning lifestyles, defining priorities and goals, and mastering steps to maintaining vitality.

The New Retirement: The Ultimate Guide to the Rest of Your Life by Jan Cullinane and Cathy Fitzgerald. Rodale Books, 2007, revised and updated ed. Vastly comprehensive, this edition features financial and tax information, a section on second homes, travel suggestions, and information about where to live, what to do, and when to do it.

Retirement Is a Full-time Job: And You're the Boss by Bonnie Louise Kuchler. Willow Creek, 2009. This lighthearted book is filled with quotes, anecdotes, and photos.

Some Useful Web Sites

AARP. *www.aarp.org.* From America's leading organization for people age fifty and older, this site provides information and education about health and wellness, leisure and fun, legislative issues, life transitions, money, work, volunteering, and computers and technology.

Money.com. *www.money.com.* In addition to covering many retirement topics such as choosing appropriate investment vehicles, setting up family trusts, and understanding the roles of pensions, 401(k)s, IRAs, and the like, this site offers retirement savings calculators, cost of living calculators, and a tool for finding the best place to retire.

Quicken.com. *www.quicken.com.* This site contains general financial information and a good selection of pages on retirement basics such as 401(k)s, pension plans, IRAs, Social Security, and a retirement planner as well as the special topics of taking care of aging parents and planning for inflation. It also offers software for retirement planning.

Social Security Retirement Planner. *www.ssa.gov.* This government site provides information on eligibility factors affecting retirement benefits, options available as you near retirement, and several benefit calculators using different retirement scenarios.

www.2young2retire.com. This site is geared toward people who are forty-five and older and are interested in new careers, businesses, volunteer work, and adventures. It features people who have made radical lifestyle and career changes as well as links to other sites on careers, learning, volunteering, and wellness.

Chapter 11: The Eleven Keys to Success

Emotional Intelligence by Daniel Goleman. Bantam Books, 1995. A popular research-based book that makes the case for emotional intelligence being the strongest indicator of human success. Emotional intelligence is defined in terms of self-awareness, altruism, personal motivation, empathy, and the ability to love and be loved.

How We Decide by Jonah Lehrer. Houghton Mifflin, 2009. This book is an insightful read about the science of decision-making.

Following Through: A Revolutionary New Model for Finishing Whatever You Start by Pete Greider and Steve Levinson. Unlimited Publishing, 2007. This book teaches different ways to understand and handle your good intentions as well as make things happen.

Learned Optimism: How to Change Your Mind and Your Life by Martin Seligman. Pocket Books, 1998. This groundbreaking classic provides a psychological discussion of pessimism, optimism, learned helplessness, and depression, and how these affect success, health, and quality of life. The book teaches how to turn pessimism into optimism with worksheet pages.

Some Useful Web Sites

Eqi.com. *www.eqi.com.* This site has dozens of articles on empathy, self-awareness, and many of the other Eleven Keys.

Helpguide.org. *http://helpguide.org.* This comprehensive nonprofit Web site with the tagline Understand, Prevent & Resolve Life's Challenges has hundreds of articles on topics such as humor, creativity, communication, and many of the other keys.

TestYourself.Psychtests. *http://testyourself.psychtests.com/testid/2092.* This Web site has a multitude of tests. The specific link here is for a thirty-five-minute test to assess your emotional intelligence.

Several Good Overview Articles

"Beginner's Guide to Being Decisive." *http://www.avani-mehta .com/2008/07/17/beginners-guide-to-being-decisive.*

Chapter 12: Job Search—the Nuts and Bolts

Job Search How-tos

Knock 'em Dead: The Ultimate Job Search Guide by Martin Yate. Adams Media, 2009. This book has been praised as one of the most comprehensive career books on the market. It is filled with interviewing strategies, Internet resources, and tools for helping job applicants stand out.

What Color Is Your Parachute? A Practical Manual for Job-Hunters and Career-Changers by Richard N. Bolles. Ten Speed Press, 2009. First published in 1970 and updated frequently, this book remains a classic in the field.

Get the Job You Want, Even When No One's Hiring by Ford R. Myers. Wiley, 2009. Written for the multitude of workers who were casualties of the 2008 recession, the book outlines the job search strategies necessary in bad economic times.

Career Coward's Guide to Changing Careers: Sensible Strategies for Overcoming Job Search Fears by Katy Piotrowski. JIST Works, 2007. Career coach Katy Piotrowski offers practical, friendly, comforting advice for the intimidated career change wannabe.

Job Hunting That Works! Find Your Next Job in a Month by Anna Boothe. CreateSpace, 2009. This concise guidebook spells out a focused and proven formula that Boothe has used in her work with the Salvation Army for finding a job as soon as possible.

A Useful Web Site

The Five O'Clock Club. *www.fiveoclockclub.com.* The Five O'Clock Club is a national outplacement and career counseling network with certified career counselors across the United States.

Branding

Me 2.0: Build a Powerful Brand to Achieve Career Success by Dan Schawbel. Kaplan, 2009. This is a logically organized, comprehensive handbook describing a four-step process for personal branding. A large focus is on blogs, podcasting, and social networking.

Career Distinction: Stand Out by Building Your Brand by William Arruda and Kirsten Dixson. Wiley, 2007. The focus of this book is to show readers how to express and manage their personal brand and the value you bring to your employer and industry.

Self Marketing Power: Branding Yourself as a Business of One by Jeff Beals. Keynote Publishing, 2008. This is an essential tool for anyone in the business world who wants to find a new job, boost revenue, start a business, or get promoted.

The Complete Idiot's Guide to Branding Yourself by Sherry Beck Paprocki. Alpha, 2009. Offering a different perspective at a time-tested business practice, Paprocki guides readers through defining and building a personal brand that is distinctive, relevant, and consistent.

Interviewing

Acing the Interview: How to Ask and Answer Questions That Will Get You the Job by Tony Beshara. AMACOM, 2008. At some point most people have been caught off guard by tough interview questions. This book takes readers through the entire process, from the initial interview to evaluating a job offer, and even into salary negotiation. *Acing the Interview* is a no-nonsense, take-no-prisoners guide to interview success.

Ask the Headhunter: Reinventing the Interview to Win the Job by Nick A. Corcodilos. Plume Books, 2007. A guide to "the new interview," a unique and aggressive method for job hunters to prepare for interviews and effectively showcase their expertise.

Job Interviews for Dummies by Joyce Lain Kennedy. For Dummies, 2008, 3rd ed. This edition provides up-to-date technological changes, interview strategies, and negotiation techniques to help job hunters land their dream job.

60 Seconds and You're Hired by Robin Ryan. Penguin Books, 2000. In this oldie-but-goodie guide, Ryan provides concise advice and easy techniques for mastering an interview.

Some Useful Web Sites

CareerJournal from the *Wall Street Journal. www.careerjournal.com.* This site provides a résumé database; lets you create a job search "agent" that searches for jobs meeting your criteria and reports results to you via e-mail; and provides salary and hiring information, job-hunting advice, tips on managing your career, and information on executive recruiters, as well as topical news stories.

HotJobs.yahoo.com. *www.hotjobs.yahoo.com.* This is one of the largest Internet job sites, with job postings in more than twenty-eight categories in the United States, Canada, and Australia. It also hosts online career expos, forums, and job fairs.

Juju. *www.job-search-engine.com/searchjob.* Not a job board but an "infomediary" Web site that searches the top three hundred U.S. and Canadian job boards in parallel and in real time. Lets you specify a variety of job criteria and locations to search in.

Monster.com. *www.monster.com.* This is a "monster" site with more than three thousand pages of career advice, résumés, and salary information, as well as a vast job-posting database. Additional features include opportunities for senior executives, advice on relocating, and a database for contractors.

JobDig. *www.jobdig.com.* This employment media company publishes local editions in more than fourteen states in print and on the Web.

Indeed.com. *www.indeed.com.* This site aggregates job postings from job sites, newspapers, associations, and company career pages. Indeed.com also releases industry trends to help job seekers and employers navigate the job market.

TheLadders.com. *www.theladders.com.* This job site allows job seekers, for a monthly subscription fee, to search for jobs that pay $100,000 or more in sales, marketing, finance, human resources, law, technology, and operations.

LinkUp. *www.LinkUp.com.* This job search engine only indexes jobs from over twenty thousand company Web sites, giving job seekers access to the purest jobs on the Web—direct from the source.

Craigslist. *www.craigslist.org.* This Web site is a centralized network of online communities featuring free online classified ads with sections devoted to jobs, résumés, housing, and for-sale services.

ReferenceUSA *www.referenceusa.com.* This Web site enables job seekers to gather information about specific companies.

Résumé Writing

How to Write and Design a Professional Resume to Get the Job: Insider Secrets You Need to Know by Dale Mayer. Atlantic Publishing, 2008. During tough economic times, a great résumé is a crucial tool for standing out among the competition. This book covers every element of creating an effective résumé.

Everything Resume Book: Create a Winning Resume That Stands Out from the Crowd by Nancy Schuman. Adams Media, 2008, 3rd ed. Schuman believes that building a strong résumé is the most important step in landing a new job. This book has more than one hundred sample résumés for a wide range of professions.

Knock 'em Dead Resumes: Features the Latest Information on Online Postings, Email Techniques, and Follow-up Strategies by Martin Yate. Adams Media, 2008. This book has been a best-seller for more than a decade, and this updated version includes new examples of résumés and a new "before" and "after" section.

An Interesting Web Site

Bakos Group. *www.800-370-jobs.com.* In addition to being "the world's largest résumé, career management, employment, and outplacement service," and providing the traditional job search capabilities, this site will give you a free critique of your résumé.

Networking

Never Eat Alone and Other Secrets to Success: One Relationship at a Time by Keith Ferrazzi. Currency Doubleday, 2005. Ferrazzi distinguishes his unique and counterintuitive perspective on networking from the usual concept of networking involving generic handshakes and handing out business cards.

Highly Effective Networking: Meet the Right People and Get a Great Job by Orville Pierson. Career Press, 2009. Pierson tells readers how to get a job without building a huge, powerful network— by using the network they already have.

Little Black Book of Connections: 6.5 Assets for Networking Your Way to Rich Relationships by Jeffrey Gitomer. Bard Press, 2006. A leading sales trainer, Gitomer offers a fresh take on networking and connecting your way to success.

The LinkedIn MBA by Sean E. Nelson. Bard Press, 2009, 2nd ed. This book is a very detailed how-to book covering strategies and tips for leveraging LinkedIn to build your network.

Make Your Contacts Count: Networking Know-how for Business and Career Success by Anne Baber. AMACOM, 2007. This book is great for networking beginners as well as a refresher for executives who are committed to proactively managing their careers.

Some Useful Web Sites

MyJobSearch.com. *www.myjobsearch.com.* This site provides information on career planning, résumé writing, interviewing, employers, negotiating, and relocation. The pages on networking are especially good, covering associations, government leaders, colleges and universities, career fairs, a people finder, and a good reading list on the topic.

Quintessential Careers. *www.quintcareers.com.* In addition to access to traditional job search and career planning information, this site provides a collection of networking resources on the Internet, general networking organizations, professional organizations and associations, women's networking and professional organizations, a reading list, and an interviewing tutorial.

LinkedIn.com. *www.linkedin.com.* The preeminent and most widely used business social networking Web site, LinkedIn provides more than eleven ways to increase your profile and expand your network rapidly.

Search Firms

Ask the Headhunter: Reinventing the Interview to Win the Job by Nick A. Corcodilos. Plume, 2007. Headhunter Corcodilos provides effective self-marketing techniques to help people locate jobs that are right for them and receive job offers. The author helps readers focus on what a job search is all about: doing a job profitably for the employer.

Index

A

Acquiescent personality, in self-
    assessment, 47, 48
Acquisitions and mergers, corporate,
    4–5, 111
Action plans, 22–23
    for "Been There, Done That, but
        Still Need to Earn" situation,
        96–101
    for "Bored and Plateaued" situation,
        140–143
    for "Bruised and Gun-shy" situation,
        120–124
    in job search, 236–237
    for "One Toe in the Retirement
        Pool" situation, 196–200
    for "Where's the Meaning?"
        situation, 83–86
    for "Yearning to Be on Your Own"
        situation, 173–181
        business plan, 274–275
        twenty-six things to do, 176–180
        vision statement, 173–174
Ads, answering, 242
Age, 6, 72, 103–104
    older workers, 194
    retirement and, 182
    (see also Baby boomers)

Age Works (Goldberg), 8
American Association of Retired
    Persons (AARP), 182, 193,
    200
Are You a Corporate Refugee? (Luban),
    102–103, 119–120
Artist's Way, The (Cameron), 81
Assertive personality, in self-assessment,
    47
Assessments (see Self-assessments)
Attitude Is Everything (Harrell), 219
Attitudes, in self-assessments, 28, 34–
    36, 107

B

Baby boomers
    as entrepreneurs, 245
    Gen Xers as viewed by, 5
    retirement and, 13–14, 189–190
        (see also "One Toe in the
            Retirement Pool" situation;
            Retirement)
    saving habits of, 8
Balance, between work and life, 7–8
Bardwick, Judith, 126
Barkley, Nella, 253
Barriers (see Roadblocks)

"Been There, Done That, but Still Need
to Earn" situation, 12, 87–101
action plan for, 96–101
questions to identify, 15–16, 21
roadblocks and opportunities, 93–96
self-assessment for, 88–93
Beliefs
company culture and, 115–118
(*see also* Values)
Bizbuysell.com, 162
Bolles, Richard, 229
"Bored and Plateaued" situation, 12–
13, 125–143
action plan for, 140–143
favorite skills and, 133–134
and finding new position in same
industry, 137–138
and focusing on world outside of
work, 138–140
questions to identify, 18–19, 21
and remembering when you weren't
bored, 135
and revitalizing current job,
135–137
roadblocks and opportunities in,
131–140
self-assessment for, 128–131
task delegation and, 134–135
Boredom, 39
lack of meaning and, 76
(*see also* "Been There, Done That, but
Still Need to Earn" situation;
"Bored and Plateaued"
situation)
Bosses
difficult, 102, 112
prospective, assessment of, 112–115
questions to ask, 118–119
Bronte, Lydia, 199
"Bruised and Gun-shy" situation, 12,
102–124
action plan for, 120–124
questions to identify, 16–17, 21

roadblocks and opportunities in,
111–120
self-assessment for, 106–111
Bureau of Labor Statistics, 9
Burnout, 4
Business, vision statement for,
173–174
Business ownership, 13, 144
business plan, 174–178
buying a preexisting business, 152,
162–167
company overview, 175
executive summary, 175
financial plan, 177–178
management plan, 176–177
marketing plan, 175–176
twenty-six things to do when starting
a business, 178–180
(*see also* "Yearning to Be on Your
Own" situation)

C

Cameron, Julia, 81
Cantor, Dorothy, 254
Career (*see* Work and career)
Cash flow, in starting own business,
170–171
Cause, contribution to, 67–68, 76
Challenges and rewards, as type of
meaning, 67
Chang, Richard, 78
Change resilience
fear of the unknown, 237, 240
in self-assessments, 28, 40–42, 110,
147
Changing lifestyle
concerns about, 77–78
as type of meaning, 67
Charity organizations, 80
Cole, Neal, 194
Company culture, 115–118, 248

Company overview, in business plan, 175
Compass Point Consulting, 27–28
Confidence, 202, 203–210
Consultants, 152
Contingency firms, 242–243
    interviews and, 247
Contingency workforce, 13
Contract employee, working as, 153–154
Contributing/making a difference, 67, 75–77
Cooper, Glen, 162
Corporate acquisitions and mergers, 4–5, 111
Corporate refugees, 102–103, 105, 119–120
Creating/innovating, as type of meaning, 68
Creativity, insecurities about, 81–82
Crystal-Barkley Guide to Taking Charge of Your Career, The (Barkley and Sandburg), 253
Curiosity, 202, 210–212, 226

decisiveness, 202, 212–214
empathy, 202, 214–216
flexibility, 202, 216
humor, 202, 217
intelligence, 201, 202, 218
optimism, 202–203, 218–222
perseverance, 203, 222–224
respect, 203, 224
self-awareness, 202, 225–227
Emotional Intelligence (Goleman), 201
Emotional personality, in self-assessment, 47, 48
Empathy, 202, 214–216
Entrepreneurship, 144
    (*see also* "Yearning to Be on Your Own" situation)
Ernst & Young, 144
Eulogy, writing own, 227–228
Executive summary, in business plan, 175
Exercise, 221
Experience, lack of, 72–74
Expressing ideals and values, as type of meaning, 67

D

Data, interest in, in self-assessment, 54, 55
Decisiveness, 202, 212–214
    in job search, 236–237
DeLeno, Bill, 112, 117–118
Discrimination, "Bruised and Gun-shy" situation and, 12, 103
Don't Stop the Career Clock (Harkness), 13

E

Eleven Keys to Success, 201–228
    confidence, 202, 203–210
    curiosity, 202, 210–212, 226

F

Facebook, 242, 246
Factual personality, in self-assessment, 47
Fairleigh Dickinson University, 5
Families and Work Institute, 7
Fast Company, 229
Favorite skills
    "Bored and Plateaued" situation and, 133–134
    in self-assessments, 43, 55–60, 147–148
Fears, 237, 240
Feedback, entrepreneurship and, 171–172

Feeling passionate, as type of meaning, 67
Filipczak, Bob, 5
Finances (*see* Money and finances)
Financial plan, in business plan, 177–178
Financial planners, 93–94, 190
FindLaw.com, 144
Flexibility, 47, 202, 216
Follow-up, in job search, 246
Fortune, 224
Franchises, 152, 159–162
Free agents (temporary workers), 13, 152–154
Futurist, 101, 145, 192

G

Gallup Poll, 189, 251
Gendron, George, 152
Generations at Work (Zemke, Raines, and Filipczak), 5
Gen Xers
  baby boomers as viewed by, 5
  as entrepreneurs, 145
Goal orientation, in self-assessments, 38, 39, 90, 109
Goals, career
  job search and, 234–236
  perseverance and, 222–224
  time frame for, 97, 98
GoDaddy.com, 176, 246
Goldberg, Beverly, 8
Goleman, Daniel, 201, 214–215, 217

H

Harkness, Helen, 13
Harrell, Keith, 219
Hewitt Associates, 7
Homestead.com, 246

Howells, John, 191
Humor, 202, 217

I

Idealist personality, in self-assessment, 46–47
Ideals, 67
  finding a company that supports, 74–75
  (*see also* Values)
Ideas, interest in, in self-assessment, 55
Incantation, positive, 207–208
Independent practitioners, 152, 154–159
Independent (temporary) workers, 13, 152, 153–154
Innovating/creating, as type of meaning, 68
Intelligence, 201, 202, 218
Interesting field or industry, as type of meaning, 67
Interests, 95
  in self-assessments, 43, 49–55, 110–111, 147
  work as separate from, 51
Interim (temporary) workers, 13, 152, 153–154
Internet
  answering ads on, 242
  résumé for, 238–239
  social networking and, 241–242, 246
  technological knowledge and, 82–83
Interviews, 243–245
  assessing job in, 118–120
  assessing prospective boss in, 112–115
  contingency and search firms and, 247
  taking notes during, 247

"In the New Land" stage, 105
"In the Wilderness" stage, 105
Introverted personality, in self-
        assessment, 46–48
IQ, 201

J

Job (*see* Work and Career)
JobDig.com, 5
Job fit, 28, 104, 116–117, 199,
        248
Job interviews (*see* Interviews)
Job search, 229–249
    company culture and, 248
    decision making and action in, 236–
        237
    most important elements of, 238–
        246
        answering Internet or newspaper
            ads, 242
        branding, 245–246
        contingency and search firms,
            242–243, 247
        follow-up, 246
        interviewing (*see* Interviews)
        networking (*see* Networking)
        résumé, 238–239, 247
    myths about, 247–248
    negotiation and, 248
    plan and goals in, 234–236
    qualifications and, 248
    relationships and, 230–231
    self-knowledge and, 231–234
    in summer or in December,
        247–248
Johnson, Spencer, 41

K

Knowledge workers, 152

L

Labor, U.S. Department of, 9, 105
Lague, Louise, 3, 4
Laughter, 217
Layoffs, 102, 104, 111, 119
    "Bruised and Gun-shy" situation and,
        12, 102–103
Learned Optimism (Seligman), 219
Learning, 211–212
    as type of meaning, 68
"Letting Go" stage, 105
Levy, Harold O., 76
Life expectancy, 8
Lifehack.org, 245
Life review assessment, 226–227
Lifestyle change
    concerns about, 77–78
    as type of meaning, 67
LinkedIn, 241, 245
Lore, Nicholas, 132
Luban, Ruth, 102–103, 105, 119–120

M

Mailboxes Etc., 160–161
Maintaining motivation, in self-
        assessments, 38, 39, 89–90, 109
Making a difference, 67, 75–77
Management, 6
Management plan, 176–177
Managing relationships, in self-
        assessments, 38, 39, 89, 108
Marincci, Steve, 222
Marketing plan, 175–176
Market research, 157–158
Meaning, 63–64
    ten types of, 67–68
    see also "Where's the Meaning?"
        situation
Mentors, 101
Mercer, 7

Mergers and acquisitions, corporate, 4–5, 111
Millennials (Gen Y), 5, 145
Million Dollar Consulting (Weiss), 159
Money and finances
    attitudes about, 94
    of baby boomers, 8
    financial planning, 93–95, 190
    pay cuts, 70–71, 94
    retirement and, 183–184, 189–190, 196
    (*see also* "Been There, Done That, but Still Need to Earn" situation)
Motivation, in self-assessments, 38, 39, 89–90, 109
MySpace, 242

N

Negative self-talk, 207–208
Negotiation, 248
Networking, 73–74, 96–101, 132–133, 239–242
    entrepreneurship and, 172
    online, 241–242
Newspaper ads, answering, 242
New York Times, 76, 145, 195
Niceness, 224
Nine Steps to Financial Freedom (Orman), 93
Nonprofit organizations, 70, 71, 80

O

Objects, interest in, in self-assessment, 55
Obstacles (*see* Roadblocks)
"One Toe in the Retirement Pool" situation, 13–14, 182–200
    action plan for, 196–200

finances and, 182–184, 189–190, 196
    questions to identify, 20–21
    and reasons for considering retirement, 182–183
    roadblocks and opportunities in, 189–196
        choosing what kind of work to do, 192–196
        choosing where to live, 191–192
        finances in, 189–190
    self-assessment for, 184–188
Online social networking, 241–242, 246
"On the Brink" stage, 105, 119–120
Opportunities, 22
    in "Been There, Done That, but Still Need to Earn" situation, 93–96
    in "Bored and Plateaued" situation, 131–140
    in "Bruised and Gun-shy" situation, 111–120
    in "One Toe in the Retirement Pool" situation, 189–196
    in "Where's the Meaning?" situation, 69–83
Optimism, 202–203, 218–222
Orman, Suze, 93, 94
Outgoing personality, in self-assessment, 46

P

Parade, 194
Partnerships, 152, 168–169
Passion, 237
    in career phases, 126
    lack of, 78–79
    perseverance and, 223
    turning into job, 139
    as type of meaning, 67
Passion Plan, The (Chang), 78

Pathfinder, The (Lore), 132
Pay decrease, in job switch, 70–71, 94
People, interest in, in self-assessment, 55
Perseverance, 203, 222–224
Personality preferences, in self-assessment, 43–49
Personal life, balance between work and, 7–8
Plateauing, 125–126
    (*see also* "Bored and Plateaued" situation)
Plateauing Trap, The: How to Avoid It in Your Career and in Your Life (Bardwick), 126
Plaxo, 242
Positive risk taking, 208–209
Problem solving
    as type of meaning, 67
    in unknown field of work, 77
Professional commitment, in self-assessments, 38, 39–40, 110
Promotions, 126

R

Rahlfs, Stephanie, 144–145
Raines, Claire, 5
Realistic career goals, 96
Realist personality, in self-assessment, 46–47, 48
Relationships
    in job search, 230–231
    in self-assessments, 38, 39, 89, 108
Researching career paths, 97
Resources, entrepreneurship and, 171–172
Resources, guide to, 256–274
Respect, 203, 224
Résumé, 238–239
    Internet, 238–239
    length of, 247

Retainer firms, 242–243
Retirement
    age at, 182
    financial aspects of, 182–184, 189–190, 196
    reasons for considering, 182–183
    Social Security and, 8, 189–190, 196
    (*see also* "One Toe in the Retirement Pool" situation)
Retirement on a Shoestring (Howells), 191
Retirement plans, 8, 189, 190
Rewards and challenges, as type of meaning, 67
Risk taking, positive, 208–209
Roadblocks, 22
    in "Been There, Done That, but Still Need to Earn" situation, 93–96
    in "Bored and Plateaued" situation, 131–140
    in "Bruised and Gun-shy" situation, 111–120
    to finding meaningful work, 69–83
        age, 71–72
        feeling that you can't make a difference, 75–77
        finding a company that supports ideals and values, 74–75
        insecurity about creativity, 81–82
        lack of passion, 78–79
        lack of specific industry experience, 72–74
        lack of time, 79–81
        lifestyle changes, 77–78
        pay decrease in job switch, 70–71
        problem-solving abilities in unknown field of work, 77
    manufactured, 132
    in "One Toe in the Retirement Pool" situation, 189–196
        choosing what kind of work to do, 192–196
        choosing where to live, 191–192
        finances in, 189–190

Roadblocks *(cont.)*
in "Yearning to Be on Your Own"
    situation, 169–173
    blending work and outside life,
        172–173
    cash flow, 170–171
    lack of support system, resources,
        and feedback, 171–172
    selling, 169–170
Robbins, Mark, 189, 190, 196
Roff, Suzanne, 27–28
Rosenbluth International, 224
Rosenkopf, Lori, 146

S

Salary.com, 251
Sales, 169–170
Sandburg, Eric, 253
Sandholtz, Kurt, 126
Search firms, 242–243
    interviews and, 247
"Seeing the Bacon" stage, 105
Self-assessments, 22, 27–42, 43–60,
        231
    attitudes in, 28, 34–36, 107
    for "Been There, Done That, but
        Still Need to Earn" situation,
        88–93
    for "Bored and Plateaued" situation,
        128–131
    for "Bruised and Gun-shy" situation,
        106–111
    change resilience in, 28, 40–42, 110,
        147
    favorite skills in, 43, 55–60, 147–
        148
    goal orientation in, 38, 39, 90, 109
    interests in, 43, 49–55, 110–111,
        147
    maintaining motivation in, 38, 39,
        89–90, 109

managing relationships in, 38, 39,
        89, 108
    for "One Toe in the Retirement Pool"
        situation, 184–188
    personality preferences in, 43–49
    professional commitment in, 38, 39–
        40, 90, 110
    self-confidence in, 38, 88, 107
    self-knowledge in, 38–39, 89, 108
    values in, 28, 29–34, 47, 64–65,
        106–107
    for "Where's the Meaning?"
        situation, 64–69
    for "Yearning to Be on Your Own"
        situation, 146–151
Self-awareness, 202, 214–215, 225–227
Self-confidence, in self-assessments, 38,
        88, 107
Self-employment, 13
    (see also "Yearning to Be on Your
        Own" situation)
Self-knowledge
    in job search, 231–234
    in self-assessments, 38–39, 89,
        108
Self-talk, negative, 207–208
Seligman, Martin, 219
Selling, 169–170
Service Corps of Retired Executives
        (SCORE), 82, 83
Skills, 76, 101, 127
    "Bored and Plateaued" situation and,
        133–134
    in career phases, 126
    favorite, 43, 55–60, 133–134
    layoffs and, 119
Smart Guide to Planning for Retirement
        (Robbins), 189, 196
Social Security, 8, 189–190, 196
Software programs, 83
Solo practitioners, 152, 154–159
    professional image and, 158–159
Solving problems

as type of meaning, 67
in unknown field of work, 77
Spontaneity, in self-assessment, 47
Structure, in self-assessment, 47, 48
Success, 144, 146
Success, keys to (*see* Eleven Keys to
    Success)
Supporting a cause, 67–68, 76
Support system, entrepreneurship and,
    171–172

T

Tasks, delegation of, 134
Teaching, 76
Technological knowledge, 82–83
Telecommuting, 6–7
Temporary workers (free agents), 13,
    152–154
Tests, self-assessment (*see* Self-
    assessments)
Thank-you notes, 246, 247
Time, lack of, 79–81
Time frame, for career goals, 97, 98
Trademarks, 176
2young2retire.com, 197

U

Umbershoot.net, 79
Unique selling proposition (USP), 174
U.S. Census Bureau, 8, 182, 191
USA Today, 5

V

Vacation policies, 7
Values
    company culture and, 115–118
    emotional personality and, 47
    expression of, as type of meaning, 67
    finding a company that supports,
        74–75
    meaning and, 64–65, 70–71
    in self-assessments, 28, 29–34, 47,
        64–65, 106–107
Verizon, 7
Vision statement, 173–174
Volunteer work, 73, 79–80

W

Weiss, Alan, 159
What Color Is Your Parachute? (Bolles),
    229
*What Do You Want to Be When You Grow
    Up?* (Cantor), 254
"Where's the Meaning?" situation, 11,
    63–86
    action plan for, 83–86
    opportunities for, 69–83
    questions to identify, 14–15, 21
    roadblocks in, 69–83
        age, 71–72
        feeling that you can't make a
            difference, 75–77
        finding a company that supports
            ideals and values, 74–75
        insecurity about creativity,
            81–82
        lack of passion, 78–79
        lack of specific industry experience,
            72–74
        lack of time, 79–81
        lifestyle changes, 77–78
        pay decrease, 70–71
        problem-solving abilities in
            unknown field of work, 77
    self-assessment for, 64–69
Who Moved My Cheese? (Johnson),
    41
Work and career, 251–252

Work and career *(cont.)*
    balance between personal life and, 7–8, 172–173
    bosses and (*see* Bosses)
    entrepreneurship and, 144
        (*see also* "Yearning to Be on Your Own" situation)
    financial planning and, 93–94
    focusing on world outside of, 138–140
    interests as separate from, 51–52
    job assessment and, 118–120
    job fit and, 28, 104, 116–117, 199, 248
    looking for (*see* Job search)
    turning passion into, 139
Work situations, 11–23
    "Been There, Done That, but Still Need to Earn," 12, 15, 16, 21, 87–101
    "Bored and Plateaued," 12–13, 18–19, 21, 125–143
    "Bruised and Gun-shy," 12, 16–17, 21, 102–124
    "One Toe in the Retirement Pool," 13–14, 20–21, 182–200
    self-assessments for (*see* Self-assessments)
    "Where's the Meaning?," 11, 21, 63–86
    "Yearning to Be on Your Own" situation, 13, 19–20, 21, 144–181
    (*see also* the specific work situations by name)
World Future Society, 101

Y

Yankelovich, 169
"Yeahbuts," 132
"Yearning to Be on Your Own" situation, 13, 19–20, 21, 144–181
    action plan for, 173–181
        business plan, 174–178
        twenty-six things to do, 176–180
        vision statement, 173–174
    entrepreneurial options and, 152–169
        buying a business, 152, 162–167
        creating a partnership, 152, 168–169
        purchasing a franchise, 152, 159–162
        working as free agent, 152–154
        working as solo practitioner, 152, 154–159
    how to know if self-employment is for you, 148–151
    questions to identify, 19–20, 21
    roadblocks and opportunities in, 169–173
        blending work and outside life, 172–173
        cash flow, 170–171
        lack of support system, resources, and feedback, 171–172
        selling, 169–170
    self-assessment for, 146–151

Z

Zemke, Ron, 5